An Introducti

An Introduction to 3D Studio

A. Yarwood

Registered Developer

Longman
Scientific &
Technical

Longman Scientific & Technical
Longman Group Limited
Longman House, Burnt Mill, Harlow
Essex CM20 2JE, England
and Associated Companies throughout the world

Copublished in the United States with
John Wiley & Sons, Inc., 605 Third Avenue, New York, NY 10158

© Longman Group Limited 1995

First published 1995

British Library Cataloguing in Publication Data
A catalogue entry for this title is available from the British Library

ISBN 0-582-24513-3

Library of Congress Cataloging-in-Publication Data
Yarwood, A. (Alfred), 1937–
    An Introduction to 3D Studio/A. Yarwood
      p. cm.
    Includes index.
    ISBN 0-470-23448-2
    1. Computer animation. 2. Autodesk 3D Studio. 3. Computer
    graphics. I. Title.
TR987.7.Y37   1995   94-29948
006.6–dc20   CIP

ISBN 0-470-23448-2 (USA only)

Set by 19 in 10/13pt Melior
Produced by Longman Singapore Publishers (Pte) Ltd.
Printed in Singapore

Contents

List of plates

Colour plates are between pages 98 and 99.

Plate I   A rendering of the three glasses scene (Chapter 2) in Wire shading

Plate II   A rendering of the three glasses scene (Chapter 2) in Flat shading

Plate III   A rendering of the three glasses scene (Chapter 2) in Phong shading

Plate IV   A rendering of Exercise 1 (Chapter 7)

Plate V   A rendering of the second example in Chapter 8

Plate VI   A rendering of the fourth example in Chapter 7

Plate VII   A rendering of an engineering component created wholly within 3D Studio

Plate VIII   A rendering of Exercise 5, Chapter 5

Plate IX   A rendering of a chair – first example in Chapter 9

Plate X   A rendering of three meshing gears constructed in AutoCAD and loaded into 3D Studio via the DXF facility – eighth example in Chapter 8

Plate XI   A rendering of a sphere onto which the Jupiter.tga file has been spherically mapped. The background is a cloud scene from the CD-ROM of 3D Studio Release 2

Preface

This book is intended only as an introductory text for those wishing to learn how to use the graphics rendering and animation package Autodesk 3D Studio®. The contents of the book are suitable for students in Further and Higher Education and for others wishing to start learning how to use this excellent rendering software package. One is not able to describe all the possibilities of constructing, rendering and animating three-dimensional models of all types in a book of this size. It is hoped however that sufficient information is included in its pages to encourage readers to experiment with the software and, as a result, wish to learn more about how to use its many facilities. 3D Studio® is a very complex package. The possibilities of producing excellent coloured graphics and animations with the aid of the software are endless.

The contents of the book are based on Autodesk 3D Studio® Release 3, although some references to Release 2 are included. In particular, materials and backgrounds in a few of the examples given in its pages are taken from the CD-ROM supplied with Release 2.

The computing requirements for the operating of 3D Studio® are described in an introductory chapter, together with an outline of the methods by which the software broadly functions. This is followed by a chapter describing the rendering in 3D Studio® of 3D solid models from DXF files of drawings constructed in AutoCAD®. A third chapter deals with the creation and rendering of 3D meshes in the 3D Editor program. The two following chapters are concerned with examples of methods for producing 3D models from the 2D Shaper and 3D Lofter programs. More examples of lofted models are then given in a further chapter. A brief description of the Materials Editor includes examples of the creation of materials for adding to 3D meshes. The final chapters deal with Projects and how the Keyframer programs can be used to develop animations. One of the difficulties in describing a software package which will produce excellent animations is that it is of course impossible to actually show an animation in the pages of a book, although the sequences of operations for producing several examples of simple animations are included in the final chapter. A glossary of computing terms, a short description of some MS-DOS commands and the use of key short-cuts in 3D Studio are described in three appendices in the final pages of the book.

The book was compiled on a 486DX2 computer built to the author's specification by the firm Dart Computers of Romsey. The line drawings throughout the book were constructed in AutoCAD for Windows. The screen dumps were taken with the aid of the Inset software Hijaak for Windows and the text compiled in the Desk Top Publishing software Pagemaker 5, working as an application in Windows 3.1. The AutoCAD® drawings were inserted from AutoCAD for Windows directly into the Pagemaker pages via the Windows Clipboard. The bitmaps from the Hijaak screen dumps were placed in the pages as required. Minor amendments to the Hijaak bitmaps were made with the aid of the Windows Paintbrush program before being placed in their positions in the Pagemaker pages.

As this book was about to be printed Release 4 of 3D Studio was published. This new release is aimed at the professional user and includes enhancements which would, in any case, have been beyond the scope of a book of this nature. Because this book was written as an introductory text for the beginner in order that they could learn the rudiments of operating the package, its contents will be as well-suited to the beginner using Release 4 of 3D Studio as for the user of Release 3.

Acknowledgements

The author wishes to acknowledge with grateful thanks the help given to him by members of Autodesk Ltd.

Trademarks

The following are registered in the U.S. Patent and Trademark Office by Autodesk, Inc.:

Autodesk®, AutoCAD®, AutoSketch®, 3D Studio®, AME®, Autodesk Animator®

IBM® is a registered trademark of the International Business Machines Corporation.

MS-DOS® is a registered trademark, and Windows™ a trademark of the Microsoft Corporation.

A. Yarwood is a Registered Applications Developer with Autodesk Ltd.

Registered Developer

CHAPTER 1

Introduction

What is Autodesk 3D Studio?

Autodesk 3D Studio is a software package published by Autodesk and designed for use with a PC or other form of desktop computer. With its aid:

1. 3D models can be constructed.
2. 3D models can be rendered to produce realistic photographic representations of solid models.
3. The rendered, photographic-like renderings can have surfaces added from a very large range which includes plastics, woods, building materials, metals etc.
4. Lighting of rendered 3D models can be arranged to produce excellent visual effects, including shadows and a variety of backgrounds.
5. 3D models can be realistically animated. The lighting effects and cameras can also be animated to give variety to the animations.
6. 3D models constructed in AutoCAD can be transported into 3D Studio via DXF files to take advantage of the rendering effects which the software can produce.

Hardware requirements

1. An IBM compatible PC (or similar) fitted with an 80386, 80486 or Pentium computer processing unit chip (CPU).
2. If the CPU chip is a 386 or 486 of the SX series, then a math coprocessor (80387 or 80487) is necessary. The 486 DX and DX2 series have a built-in math coprocessor as part of the CPU chip. The Weitek 3167 math coprocessor can also be added to those computers in which it can be fitted.
3. A hard disk with at least 24 Mbyte free space.
4. At least 8 Mbytes random access memory (RAM). More will produce faster rendering of large models.

5. MS-DOS 3.3 or later. MS-DOS 5.0 or later is preferable.
6. A monitor of at least VGA performance, preferably higher.
7. A mouse for use as a selection device, although a digitizing tablet can also be used.
8. A CD-ROM drive to allow access to a large library of texture maps and other files. 3D Studio will operate however without access to the files available on the CD-ROM supplied with the package when purchased.
9. A 3.5 inch or 5.25 inch floppy disk drive to allow the reader to save files from constructions and renderings constructed with the aid of the software.
10. A hardware lock ('dongle') supplied with the software and fitted in a parallel port. The software will not work without the hardware lock.

Starting up 3D Studio

It is assumed the reader will be working with an IBM compatible personal computer (PC) working with MS-DOS. It should be noted here that if working in Windows 3D Studio will only operate as a DOS window. Once the 3D Studio software files have been loaded into the computer's hard disk – normally in a directory named either 3DS or 3DS3, the package can usually be started up by typing 3ds at the MS-DOS prompt **C:\>** from the keyboard, followed by pressing the *Return* (or *Enter*) key of the keyboard – as follows:

C:\> *enter* 3ds *Return*

and the 3D Studio files load into the computer. When fully loaded, the monitor screen appears as shown in Fig. 1.1 with the program **3D Editor** on the screen.

Fig. 1.2 names the various parts of the **3D Editor** screen:

Menu bar or Status line: When the cursor arrow is positioned in the menu bar, by moving the mouse, the names of the four pull-down menus appear. When creating models, the *x,y,z* coordinate position of the intersection of cursor lines appears.

Program title: There are six program screens. The name of the program appears at the top of the command column. The screen in Fig. 1.2 is the **3D Editor**. The other five programs are: **2D Shaper**; **3D Lofter**; **Keyframer**; **Materials Editor**; **Network**. Except for the **Network** program, these will be described later as the methods of working in each program are described.

Viewports: On start-up, the **3D Editor** appears with four viewports. If a model is created in any of the viewports, three other views of the

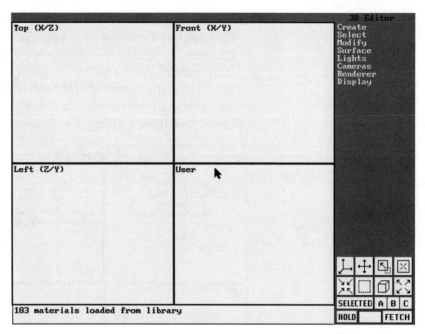

Fig. 1.1 The **3D Editor** showing on starting up 3D Studio

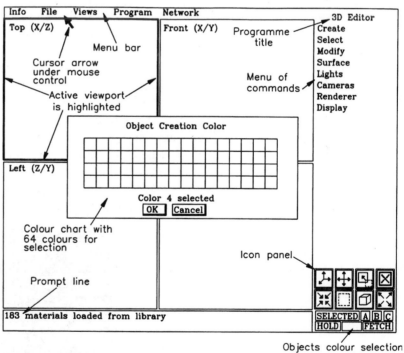

Fig. 1.2 The parts of the **3D Editor** screen

model will appear in the other three viewports. The active viewport in which a model is being created is selected by a *left-click* of the mouse in the required viewport. When a viewport is active, its edges are highlighted.

Menu of commands: The names of the menu commands appearing in the **Command column** on the right of the screen on start-up in each program, have their own sub-menus. The names of the sub-menus for **Create** of the **3D Editor** program are shown in Fig. 1.3. When three full stops appear after the sub-menu name, further sub-menus are associated with the command. Note that **Box** and **Vertex** do not have these three full stops, so have no sub-menus of their own.

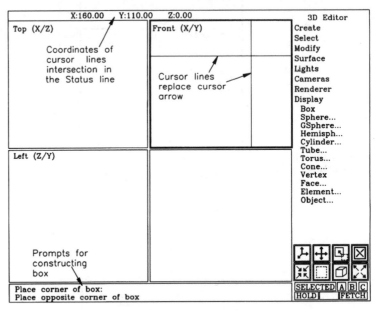

Fig. 1.3 Selecting **Box** from **Create** in the **3D Editor** screen

Icon panel: Each program screen has its own icon panel. These are largely similar to each other, but with some differences as will be explained later when other programs are discussed. An enlarged view of the icon panel for the **3D Editor** program is given in Fig. 1.4. An icon is selected and highlighted by moving the arrow cursor over the required icon, followed by a *left-click* of the mouse.

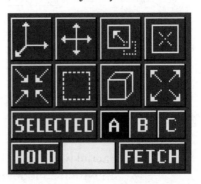

Fig. 1.4 The **icon** panel of the **3D Editor**

Prompt line: Prompts will appear in this area informing the operator of the next step to be taken to produce the result based on the selected command as construction proceeds. As the action suggested by the prompt is acted upon, further prompts will appear until the action is completed.

The selection device

This will usually be a mouse with two buttons, such as the Microsoft (or compatible) mouse. Command names, the position of points in the viewports and features from dialogue boxes are selected by moving the current cursor to the name, position or feature and pressing the left hand button of the mouse. This will be described as a *left-click*.

Message boxes

Information about methods of operation of commands, warnings and methods of setting parameters will appear in message boxes to assist the operator in creating models and renderings. There are three types of message boxes:

Warning or Alert boxes: An example is shown in Fig. 1.5. In this example, a *left-click* on **Files** in the **Menu bar**, followed by a *left-click* on **Quit** in the resulting pull-down menu, brought up the warning box. A *left-click* on **Yes** would result in leaving the 3D Studio program.

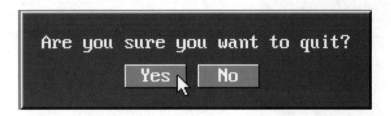

Fig. 1.5 An alert message box

Decision box: An example is given in Fig. 1.6. In this example a list of the available *.3ds files appears in the list box of the message box. A decision to select ADLOGO.3DS has been made. A *left-click* on **OK** in the message box would bring the ADLOGO model into the viewports.

Dialogue box: An example is given in Fig. 1.7. Selections as to the settings for Camera01 can be made in this dialogue box.

Viewports

All constructions in 3D Studio are carried out in viewports. As mentioned earlier, on start-up, the 3D Editor screen appears showing four viewports – Fig. 1.1. The start-up settings would show the following views in the viewports:

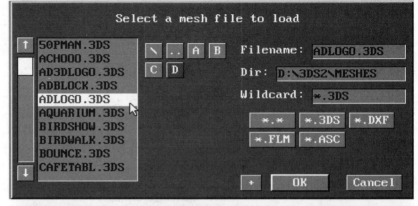

Fig. 1.6 A message box in which a decision can be made

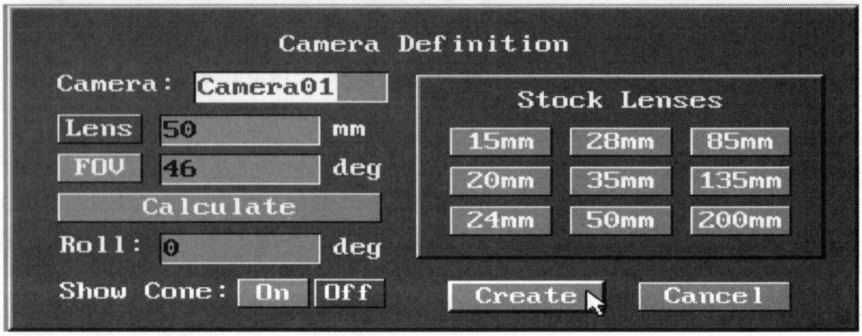

Fig. 1.7 A message box in which settings can be made: a dialogue box

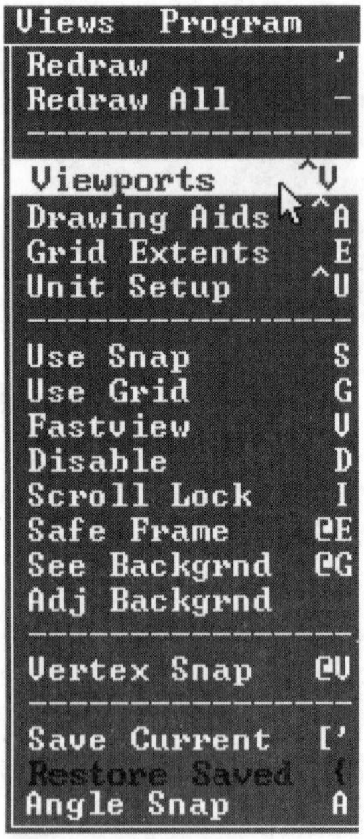

Fig. 1.8 Selecting **Viewports** from the **Views** pull-down menu

Top left: A view from above – a plan view.

Top right: A view from the front – a front view.

Bottom left: A view as seen from the left – an end view.

Bottom right: A user view – pictorial isometric view in parallel projection.

The number of viewports, and the position and view in each can be changed as follows:

1. *Left-click* on **Views** in the **Menu bar**. The **Views** pull-down menu appears – Fig. 1.8.
2. *Left-click* on **Viewports** in the pull-down menu. The **Select the viewport division method** message box appears – Fig. 1.9.
3. *Left-click* the desired viewport settings – it highlights.
4. Select which view is required in each viewport – first *left-click* in the box showing the name of the view, followed by a *left-click* in the box showing the selected viewport layout. In Fig. 1.9 – a four-viewport setting has been selected with:

Top viewport: View from left.

Middle viewport: View from front.

Lower viewport: User, showing a pictorial view.

Main viewport: View from top.

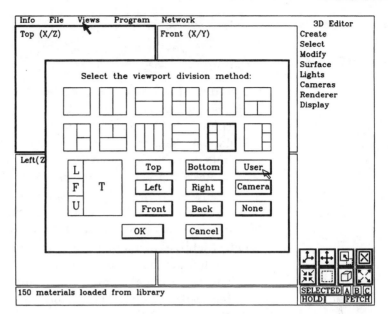

Fig. 1.9 The **Select the viewport division method** dialogue box

Fig. 1.10 shows a 3D model constructed in AutoCAD and loaded into the 3D Editor using the start-up screen viewport settings. The solid model drawing was first saved in AutoCAD as a data interchange file (DXF), then loaded into 3D Studio as a DXF file via the **File** pull-down menu.

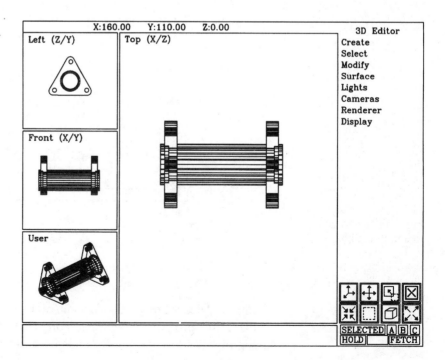

Fig. 1.10 A DXF file of a solid model constructed in AutoCAD and loaded into 3D Studio

Dialogue boxes

Fig. 1.11 gives the names of various parts of message boxes. The main features in message boxes are:

Box title: At the top of each message box as it appears on screen.

List box: Contains a list of the features – files, finishes, textures, colours, lights etc., available for selection by the operator.

Slider bar: Place the cursor under mouse control in the slider bar and hold down the left mouse button. Move the bar up or down and the names of the features in the list box move in response. *Left-click* on the upper arrow moves the list up one name; *left-click* on the lower arrow moves the names down one name. Hold the mouse button down on an arrow and the list moves continuously up or down.

Entry fields: When a name is selected from the List box, it is highlighted and the name usually appears in a field name box. Or – the name (if known) can be entered from the keyboard. Some Entry field boxes will only take figures.

Radio buttons: When there is a possible choice between e.g. disk drives or types of files, when a button is selected *(left-click)* that button becomes highlighted and all others will be off.

Exit buttons: *Left-click* on **OK** to accept settings made in a dialogue box or the messages in warning boxes. A *left-click* on **Cancel** and the box disappears from screen without any setting having been made (or accepted). Some warning boxes will contain **Yes** or **No** instead of **OK** and **Cancel**.

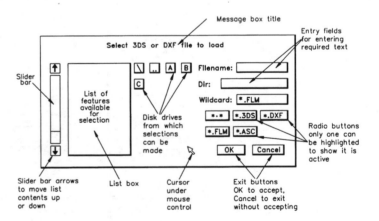

Fig. 1.11 Details of features in a message box

The icon panel

Fig. 1.12 describes the use for each of the icons in the icon panel of the **3D Editor** program screen. An icon is selected by a *left-click*. Its box highlights showing that it is has been selected. When a viewport is

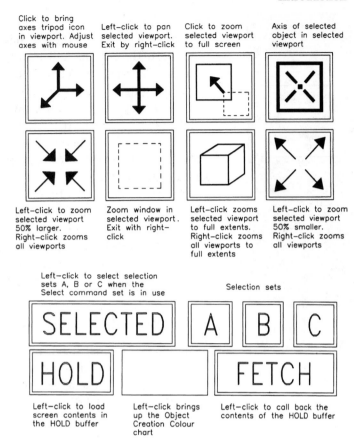

Fig. 1.12 The icon panel of the **3D Editor** program, showing the uses for each of the icons

active a left-click on an icon in the icon panel activates the action of the icon within that viewport.

There are several methods of selecting the icon functions:

1. A *left-click* usually activates the action of the icon in the active viewport.
2. A *right-click* activates the action in all viewports when the **Zoom** icons have been selected, except that which zooms with a window.
3. The action of the **Zoom window** and the **Pan** icons are cancelled with a *right-click*.
4. When the tripod icon (top left) is in action, the coordinate axes of the tripod can be rotated by movement of the mouse. When a *right-click* is given, the viewport in which the tripod was used changes to become a **User** viewport with the contents of that viewport seen in a parallel isometric view, based on the positions of the coordinate axes as selected from the tripod.

In addition to the icons the icon panel contains a number of buttons: **SELECTED**, **A**, **B**, **C**, **HOLD** and **FETCH**:

Fig. 1.13 The **Surface** command set of the **3D Editor**

SELECTED: Associated with the **Select** commands in the **3D Editor** command column. When a **Select** command is active, a *left-click* on one of the buttons **A**, **B** or **C** allows a selection set to be held under an **A**, a **B** or a **C** set. When an object or part of an object is selected, it highlights to a red colour. If, after a selection has been made, it is followed by a *left-click* on one of three buttons – e.g. on **A**, the selected parts can be recalled by a *left-click* on the **A** button. Three separate selection sets can be made with the aid of the three buttons. An example from the **Select** command sets is given in Fig. 1.13.

HOLD and FETCH: A *left-click* on **HOLD** saves the contents of the screen in a special holding buffer. This will allow further construction to continue on screen. If the further construction proves to be incorrect, the contents of the holding buffer can be re-called by a *left-click* on the **FETCH** button. The operator is advised to use these two buttons frequently because there is no **UNDO** button in the **3D Editor**, although there are **UNDO** but-tons in other programs.

Three-dimensional coordinates

A 3D model is constructed on *the default X,Y,Z* coordinates in 3D Studio. See Fig. 1.3 in which the coordinates of the position of the cursor lines are showing in the Status line. Taking the model constructed in the **3D Editor** shown in Fig. 1.15 as an example, the

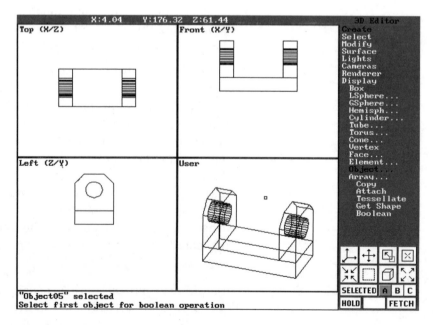

Fig. 1.14 A simple model constructed in the **3D Editor** of 3D Studio

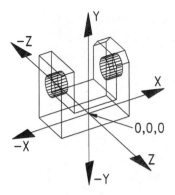

coordinate axes of the model in relation to the *X,Y,Z* axes as shown in Fig. 1.15 are such that:

1. The model is standing on the *X,Z* plane.
2. The *X,Y* plane passes through the vertical centre plane of the model.
3. The vertical *Y,Z* plane passes through the centre of the model.

The reasons for these positions of the three coordinate planes is shown in Fig. 1.16. The model was constructed in the **3D Editor** with the coordinate axes in the positions set when 3D Studio is started up.

Fig. 1.15 The positions of the *X,Y,Z* axes of the model shown in Fig. 1.14

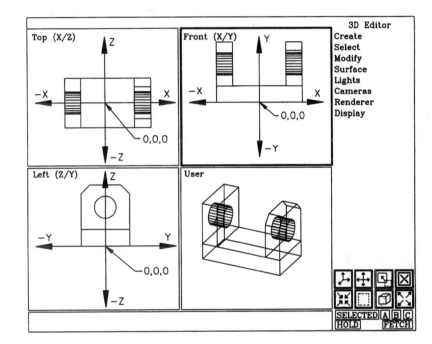

Fig. 1.16 The positions of the *X,Y,Z* axes in the viewports of the **3D Editor** screen for Fig. 1.14

Notes

1. The units of the coordinates have no equivalent in standard measurements such as millimetres or inches. They do, however allow constructions to be carried out in unit equivalents – e.g. the model in Fig. 1.14 is 170 units high, representing a drawing of an actual object which could be 170 mm high.
2. A *left-click* on **Drawing Aids** in the **View** pull-down menu, brings up the **Snap Spacing:** dialogue box. Fig. 1.17 shows the settings for this model.

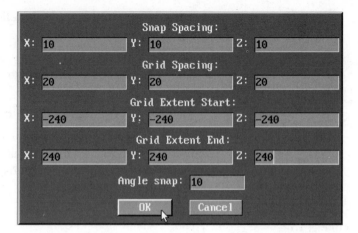

Fig. 1.17 The Grid and Snap settings for the model Fig. 1.14

3. Fig. 1.18 is a pictorial view of the **3D Editor** screen in which the model was constructed. In Fig. 1.18 it has been assumed that all features behind the screen cannot be seen.

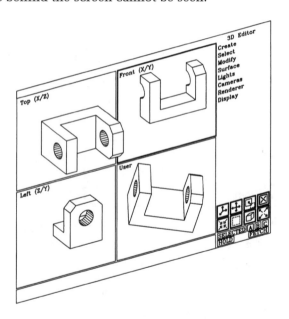

Fig. 1.18 A pictorial view of the model Fig. 1.13

Keyboard short-cuts

There are two methods by which some of the features can be called when working in 3D Studio – by selection (*left-clicks*) of the mouse on names in pull-down menus, or by pressing certain keys on the keyboard. Some of the key-stroke 'short-cuts' for the features mentioned in this chapter are:

Fig. 1.19 The **File** pull-down menu

Ctrl/A: Brings up the **Snap Spacing** dialogue box.
Ctr/V: Brings up the **Select the viewport division method** dialogue box.
F, T, L, U: In any viewport – sets the viewport to Front, Top, Left or User respectively.
G: Set Grid.
Q: Quit from 3D Studio, followed by a **Y** (for Yes).
S: Set Snap.

Note: The key-stroke shortcuts are shown against names in the pull-down menus.

Constructing three-dimensional models

Construction of 3D models in 3D Studio often starts with the drawing of shapes in the 2D Shaper program. The shapes so drawn are then transferred to the **3D Lofter** program for changing to 3D models, and then perhaps passed on to the **3D Editor** program for further editing and rendering.

Saving at intervals

When working in 3D Studio, it is advisable to save your work at regular intervals in order to avoid losing the work you have constructed. Failure to observe this rule may result in the loss of many hours of work if a fault occurs in the working of the software or during a failure of power to the computer in use.

To save your work, *left-click* on **Save** in the File pull-down menu (Fig. 1.19). The **Select a mesh file to save** dialogue box appears (Fig. 1.20). *Enter* or select the required filename and *left-click* on **OK** to save the file. Saving your work at regular fifteen or thirty minutes intervals is suggested.

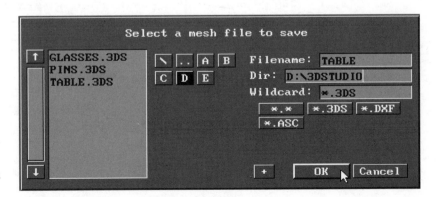

Fig. 1.20 **The Select a mesh file to save** dialogue box

Cursors

In addition to the arrow cursor shown in several illustrations in this chapter other cursors will be seen in 3D Studio. Fig. 1.22 shows this

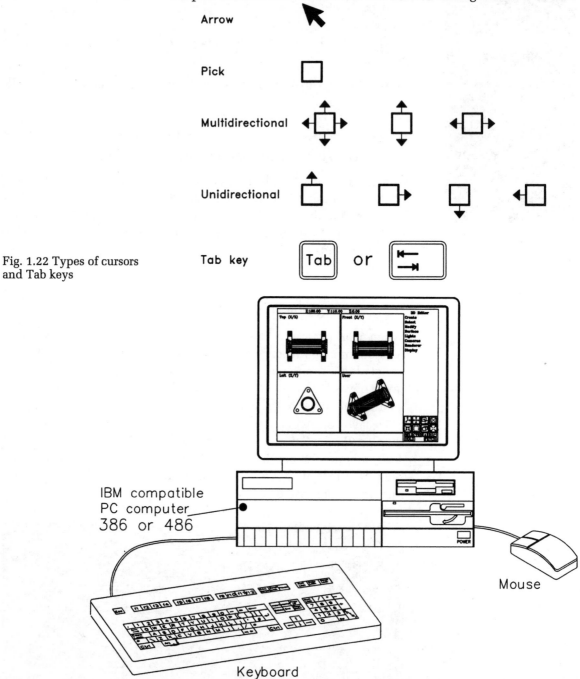

Fig. 1.22 Types of cursors and Tab keys

Fig. 1.23 An example of a hardware computer set up for 3D Studio

variety. The multidirectional and unidirectional types of cursor are changed by pressing the Tab key of the keyboard, which is marked either with the word Tab or with two arrows as shown.

Questions

1. How many programs are there in 3D Studio? Can you name them?
2. What is meant by 3D coordinates?
3. What is meant by the term 'rendering'?
4. How are the number and positions of viewports set in the **3D Editor**?
5. What shows on the **Menu bar** when the cursor arrow is placed in the bar?
6. What shows in the **Status bar** when a **Box** is being created in the **3D Editor**?
7. What is the icon panel?
8. Experiment with icons in the icon panel using both *left-clicks* and *right-clicks*. What happens in each case?
9. What are the three types of message box in 3D Studio?
10. State one method by which a 3D model from AutoCAD can be loaded into the **3D Editor**.

CHAPTER 2

3D Editor – Rendering DXF files from AutoCAD

Introduction

The settings for lights, cameras, materials and backgrounds for rendering in 3D Studio are made in the **3D Editor**. Once the settings have been made, rendering is also started in the **3D Editor**. To demonstrate the methods of setting the parameters for the rendering of a 3D solid model, three solid models constructed in AutoCAD and saved as DXF files (Data Interchange File format) will be described. DXF files of solid model drawings, whether constructed in AutoCAD or in any other CAD software system which supports both 3D modelling and DXF, can be loaded directly into the **3D Editor** of 3D Studio. The first example – a rendering of three wine glasses resting on a table top, will be described in detail. The descriptions of the other two examples – a table made from ash and an engineering component assembly – will be limited to stating the number of lights, the materials and the backgrounds allocated to the parts of the two models.

Method of describing the selection of commands

In order to show which command is chosen from those in the command columns of any of the four programs (modules) in 3D Studio, the following type of sequence description will be used throughout this book:

Surface/Material.../Get library

This means *left-click* on **Surface** in the command column, followed by a *left-click* on **Material...**, followed by a *left-click* on **Get Library**. This particular sequence will bring the **Select a material library to load** dialogue box on screen. In the dialogue box, a *left-click* on **ACADCLR.MLI** in the list box will bring the name of that file into the **Filename:** box. A *left-click* on **OK** will load the library file into memory. A *double-left-click* on the name in the list box would have the same effect.

An example rendering – the file glasses.dxf

Fig. 2.1 is a drawing of a 3D solid model drawn in AutoCAD using the **REVSURF** and **3DFACE** command features of the software. The drawing was saved as a DXF file with the filename **GLASSES.DXF**. Each glass was drawn in a different colour and the surface on which they stand was drawn in yet another colour. Before loading a DXF file into 3D Studio such as this one – drawn in several colours – it is advisable to first load the material library **ACADCLR.MLI** into memory as described above – Fig. 2.2. As its name implies, this library file loads into memory materials for 255 colours. Then, no matter which colours were used when constructing the drawing in AutoCAD, a material colour will be available for the various parts of the drawing (its objects) constructed in AutoCAD.

The sequence of commands used to render the glasses.dxf file in 3D Studio is as follows.

Note: Watch the prompt line at the foot of the **3D Editor** screen as each part of the sequence is followed.

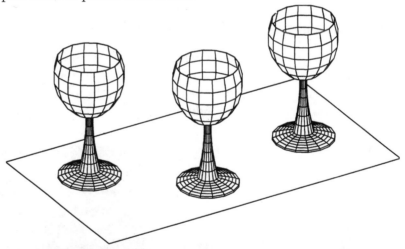

Fig. 2.1 The solid model drawing from AutoCAD

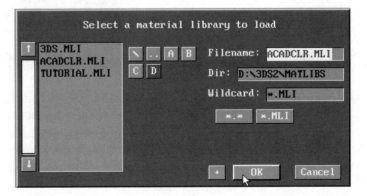

Fig. 2.2 The **Select a material library to load** dialogue box

1. **Surface/Material.../Get Library**. *Double-left-click* on the material library **ACADCLR.MLI** in the **Select a material library to load** dialogue box which appears. This loads the colour library.

2. *Left-click* on **File** in the **Menu bar**. *Left-click* on **Load** in the pull-down menu. In the dialogue box **Select a mesh file to load** – Fig. 2.3 – *left-click* in the ***.DXF**, followed by a *double-left-click* on **GLASSES** in the list box.

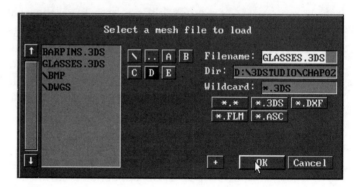

Fig. 2.3 The **Select a mesh file to load** dialogue box

3. The **Loading DXF File** dialogue box appears – Fig. 2.4. *Left-click* on the **Color** button, because the AutoCAD drawing was constructed in different colours for each glass and for the surface on which they stand. The **Color** button highlights. *Left-click on* **OK**. The DXF file loads to appear in the four viewport layout of the **3D Editor** – Fig. 2.5.

Fig. 2.4 The **Loading DXF File** dialogue box

4. **Lights/Ambient**. Set the **L** slider to 140. Note that the **B**, **G** and **R** sliders automatically adjust to the same figure of 140. *Left-click* on **OK** in the **Ambient Light Definition** dialogue box.

5. *Right-click* twice in the **Zoom out** icon box in the icon panel – all four viewports zoom out sufficiently to allow lights and camera to be placed.

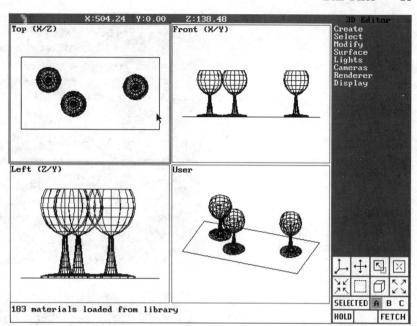

Fig. 2.5 The loaded DXF file
GLASSES.DXF

6. **Lights/Omni.../Create**. *Left-click* in the **Top (X/Z)** viewport to place the **Omni** light.

7. *Left-click* on **Create** in the **Light Definition** dialogue box to accept the default values for the light (Light01).

8. **Lights/Omni.../Move**. Move the Omni light to a suitable position – you may have to work in several viewports for this. The best position is immediately above the glasses.

9. **Lights/Spot.../Create**. Place a spotlight and its target following the prompts in the prompt line. Set the **L** slider to 255 in the **Spot Light Definition** dialogue box which appears, noting that the **R**, **G** and **B** sliders automatically adjust to the same figure. *Left-click* on **OK**.

10. **Light/Spot.../Create**. Place a second spotlight and its target. In the **Spot Light Definition** dialogue box which re-appears, set the **RGB** sliders as suggested in Fig. 2.6, followed by a *left-click* on **OK**.

11. **Lights/Spot.../Move**. In any of the viewports move the two spotlights and their target positions to suitable positions.

12. **Cameras/Create**. Place a camera near to the first spotlight, with its target in the scene.

13. In the **Camera Definition** dialogue box (Fig. 2.7), *left-click* in the **50 mm** box, followed by a *left-click* on **Create**.

14. *Left-click* in the **User** viewport, then *enter* the letter **c** at the keyboard. The name of the viewport changes to **Camera01** and the viewport shows the scene as it appears from that camera.

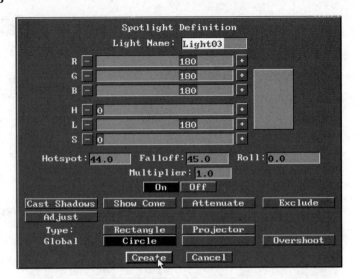

Fig. 2.6 The **Spot Light Definition** dialogue box for **Light03**

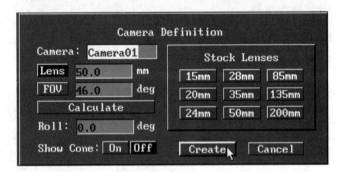

Fig. 2.7 The **Camera Definition** dialogue box

15. **Cameras/Move**. Adjust the position of the camera until the scene in the **Camera01** viewport is to your liking. You may have to work in more than one viewport for this.

16. **Surface/Materials.../Get Library**. Change the loaded library to **3DS.MLI** in the **Select a materials library to load** dialogue box.

17. **Surface/Materials.../Choose**. In the **Materials Selector** dialogue box – Fig. 2.8 – *left-click* on **BLUE GLASS** in the list box, followed by a *left-click* on **OK**.

18. **Surface/Material.../Assign.../Object**. *Left-click* on the glass to which the material is to be applied. A message box appears – Fig. 2.9. *Left-click* on **OK**, if the selection is as is required.

19. Repeat item **18** to assign **RED GLASS**, **GREEN GLASS** and **WOOD MED.ASH** materials to the other objects in the scene.

20. **Surface/Mapping.../Adjust.** Move and adjust the position of the default **Planar** mapping icon which appears in the viewports. Use **Surface/Mapping.../Adjust.../Region Fit** to fit the **Planar** mapping icon around objects in a scene.

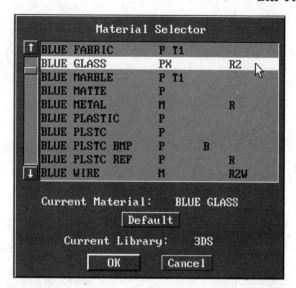

Fig. 2.8 The **Materials Selector** dialogue box

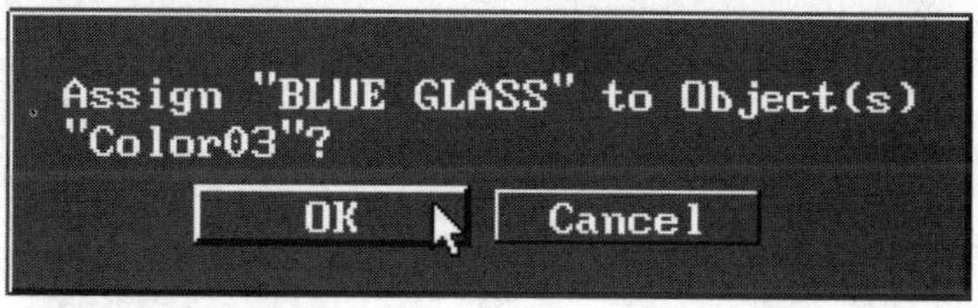

Fig. 2.9 The **Assign material** message box

21. **Surface/Mapping.../Apply Obj.** *Left-click* on each of the three glasses in turn to apply mapping – Fig. 2.10.
22. **Surface/Mapping.../Adjust.../Rotate**. Rotate and adjust the size of the mapping icon to the table top, followed by **Surface/Mapping.../Apply Obj.** and *left-click* on the table top. Note – when rotating the mapping icon, follow the degrees angle showing in the Status line in order to rotate exactly to 90º.
23. **Renderer/Setup.../Background**. *Left-click* in the **Solid Color** box in the **Background Method** dialogue box (Fig. 2.11) and set the colour in the **Define Solid Color** dialogue box – Fig. 2.12, followed by a *left-click* on **OK**.
24. **Render/Render View**. *Double-left-click* in the **Camera01** viewport and rendering commences.

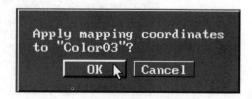

Fig. 2.10 The **Apply mapping** message box

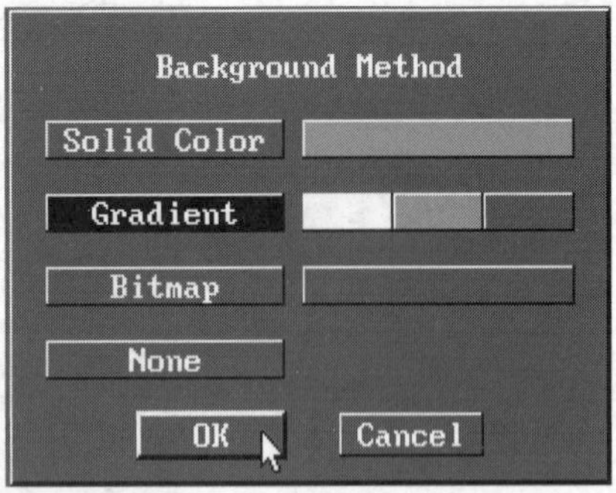

Fig. 2.11 Setting the background in the **Background Method** dialogue box

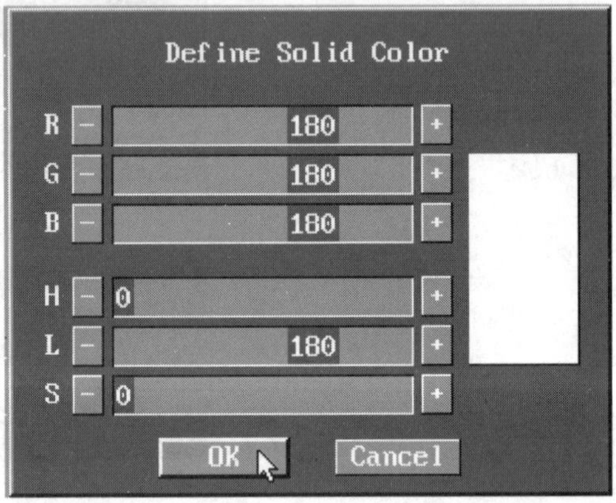

Fig. 2.12 The **Define Solid Color** dialogue box for setting the background colour

25. **Renderer/Setup.../Options**. The **Render Options** dialogue box appears (Fig. 2.13). In the dialogue box, check that the **Save Last Image** button **Yes** is set to show it highlighted. If it is not then *left-click* on the button. Failure to set this button will result in your not being able to save the last image after rendering has been completed.

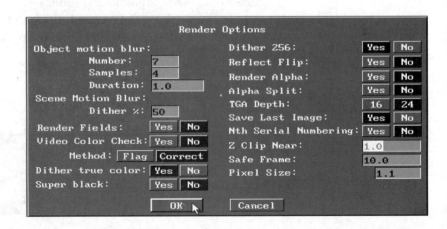

Fig. 2.13 The **Render Options** dialogue box

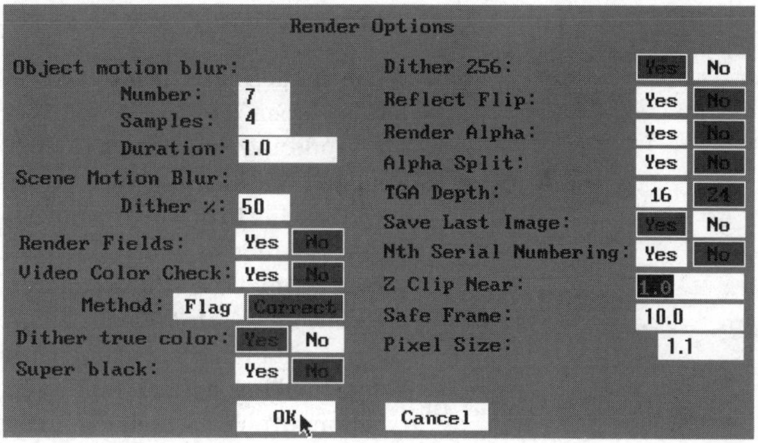

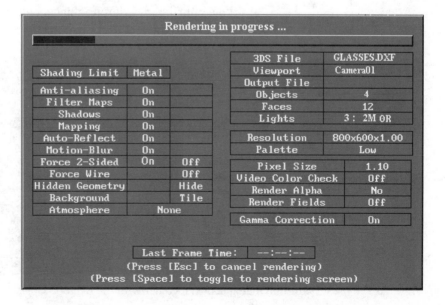

Fig. 2.14 The **Render Options** dialogue box

26. In the **Render Still Image** dialogue box – Fig. 2.14 – set **Shading Limit** to **Phong** and **Anti-aliasing**, **Filter Maps**, **Shadows**, **Mapping**, **Auto-Reflect** and **Force 2-sided** by *left-clicks* in the **On** buttons, followed by a *left-click* on the **Render** button.

27. The **Rendering in Progress...** message box appears – Fig. 2.15 – showing the stage to which rendering has proceeded. Rendering inevitably takes some time, the faster the computer, the shorter the time it takes. For this particular rendering, working on a 486DX2 machine with 16 Mbytes of RAM, rendering took about 4 minutes. The actual time taken in rendering will show in the Prompt line of the **3D Editor** when back in the program.

Fig. 2.15 The **Rendering in Progress...** message box

Notes

1. When rendering is completed, a *right-click* brings back the **3D Editor** screen.
2. The rendering time shows in the Prompt line.
3. **Renderer/View.../Save Last** allows the last rendered image to be saved as a file to disk in the **Save last image to file** dialogue box, in which the rendering can be saved. The file can be called back to screen at any time with **Renderer/View.../Image** which brings on the **View image file** dialogue box, from which saved tga files can be called back to the screen at any time.
4. Before making a final rendering, it is advisable to check the positions of objects, their colours, materials and lighting by rendering to **Flat** and with all the **Off** buttons set. A rendering to these parameters will take about 25% of the time when **Phong** shading and other parameters are set **On**. But the rendering will allow you to check whether your scene is ready for a final rendering.
5. The reader is advised to experiment with the settings in the various dialogue boxes in order to practise the results of various settings. As an example – in the **Light Definition** dialogue box (Fig. 2.16) check what happens when the buttons **Exclude**, **Attenuation**, **Tag** etc. are set. Practise different settings in the **Render Still Image** dialogue box. Such practice will allow the reader to become more proficient in operating with the software.
6. A *left-click* in the white button at the bottom of the icon panel brings up the **Object Creation Color** box from which the colour of an object can be set (Fig. 1.2, page 3). Make use of this facility, not only for the colouring of different objects before they are created, but also because of the fact that the object takes on the colour's name.

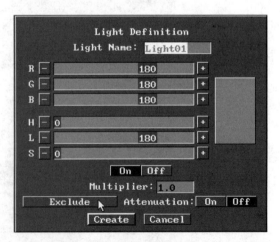

Fig. 2.16 The **Light Definition** dialogue box, together with the **Exclude Objects** box

Fig. 2.17 The **File** pull-down menu with **Save** highlighted by being selected

7. Note that the **Object Creation Color** box only appears with its 64 colours if the screen is set to work with at least 256 colours. A 16-colour screen will produce only a white box without other colours.

Saving your work

As stated in Chapter 1, it is advisable to save your work at regular intervals – at say 15 to 30 minute intervals. To save a file which has had rendering lights, cameras, materials and mapping included, save the results as a file with the extension *.3ds*. To save a mesh file (as it is called), *left-click* on **File** in the **Menu bar**, followed by a *left-click* on **Save** – Fig. 2.17. The **Select a mesh file to save** dialogue box then appears – Fig. 2.18 – in which disk drives can be selected and filenames entered.

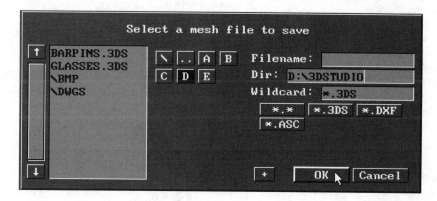

Fig. 2.18 The **Select a mesh file to save** dialogue box

Lights

Three types of light can be added to a scene – **Ambient**, **Omni** and **Spot**. Of these the **Ambient** light adds a general overall lighting to the screen. A scene with only ambient light will render only as grey masses, with little definition of the shapes in the scene. An **Omni** light sheds light in all directions as from a sphere. **Onmi** lighting could be compared with the light from an electric light bulb without a shade. A **Spot** light casts a beam of light which is directional and which can be adjusted as to the size of the beam (its cone) and the size and position of its central 'hotspot'. The colour of any of these three types of lighting can be adjusted by the **Red**, **Green** and **Blue** sliders in their respective dialogue boxes. A box to the right of the **RGB** sliders in the dialogue boxes will show the resulting colour. In addition the **Hue**, **Luminance** and **Saturation** of the light can be adjusted in the **H**, **L** and **S** slider bars. Any adjustment of these three sliders will also show up in the colour displayed in the colour boxes of the respective dialogue boxes. Fig. 2.6

on page 20 shows the **Spotlight definition** dialogue box with its two sets of three sliders with which lights are adjusted. The dialogue boxes for the other two types of lighting are similar, except that the **Hotspot**, **Falloff** and **Show Cone** boxes are not available in the **Ambient** and **Omni** lights dialogue boxes.

Positioning lights in a scene

Fig. 2.19 shows three of the viewports of the three glasses scene in the **3D Editor**. These show a generally reasonable method of position lights and cameras for the rendering of any scene. The lights as shown in Fig. 2.19 are:

Ambient: not seen in the viewports. Set to an average **RGB** to give a dim overall light.

Omni: (Light01). Immediately above the scene. Full white light – all **RGB** sliders set to 255 (maximum).

Spot: (Light02). In front, to the left and slightly above the scene. **RGB** sliders all set to 255.

Spot: (Light03). In front to the right and above the scene but not as high as Light02. **RGB** sliders each set to 150.

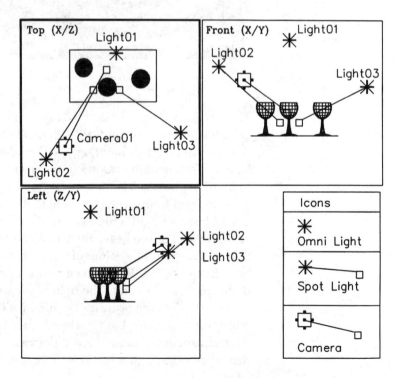

Fig. 2.19 The position of lights in the three glasses scene

Falloff and Hotspot of Spotlights

Fig. 2.20 shows one of the viewports from the **3D Editor** screen showing the three glasses scene. The **Show Cone: On** button for each of the **Spot** lights has been set with a *left-click* in the button in the **Spotlight definition** dialogue boxes for the two lights. The cones are adjusted with **Lights/Spot.../Falloff** and **Light/Spot.../Hotspot** to the shapes and sizes shown in Fig. 2.20.

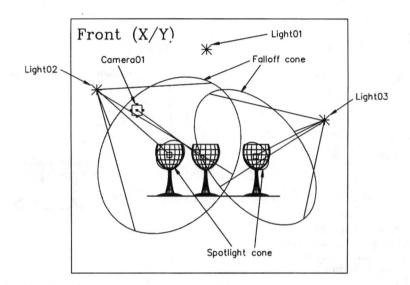

Fig. 2.20 **Falloff** and **Hotspot** cones of **Spotlights** in the three glasses scene.

Notes

1. Although the above outlines a general form of lighting which will produce reasonable results, many other ways of positioning lights are possible. The reader is advised to experiment.
2. A spotlight placed behind and below a scene will often enhance the outlines of objects in the scene.
3. A spotlight placed to the rear and above the scene sometimes enhances lighting.
4. Additional light can be added to any scene to give desired effects. For example, a spotlight with a narrow **Falloff** cone and a **Hotspot** cone of the same size as the **Falloff**, can give a distinct highlighting at the spot at which the light is directed.

Cameras

Several cameras can be included with a scene in the **3D Editor**. Several cameras will allow the scene to be viewed from a variety of positions.

In the three glasses scene, only one camera has been included. This has been placed in a position similar to the main spot (Light01). Its position is adjusted until the scene showing in the **Camera** viewport is thought to be suitable. The cone of the camera will show in the viewports if the **Show Cone: On** button is selected when setting the parameters for the camera in the **Camera definition** dialogue box. Fig. 2.21 shows the cone appearing for **Camera01** when this button is set on.

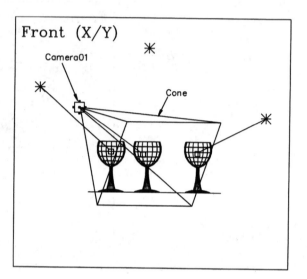

Front (X/Y)

Camera01

Cone

Fig. 2.21 The camera of the three glasses scene with **Show Cone** set in the **Camera definition** dialogue box

Mapping

When choosing materials to be applied to objects in a scene, it will be noted that against the materials name in the **Materials Selector** dialogue box, a number of letters and/or figure will be seen against some of the material names (Fig. 2.2, page 17). A possible thirteen letters or figures may be included with any of the materials. There are in fact thirteen columns next to the name of each material showing its characteristics. What the letters or figures in these thirteen columns show is given below:

Column 1: Shading when rendering – **F**(lat); **G**(ourand); **P**(hong); **M**(etal).

Column 2: **X** only if transparency is greater than **0**.

Column 3: **T** if the material is assigned a **Texture#1** map.

Column 4: **T** if the material is assigned a **Texture#2** map.

Column 5: **O** if assigned an **Opacity** map.

Column 6: **B** if assigned a **Bump** map.

Column 7: **S** if the material is assigned a **Specular** map.
Column 8: **H** if the material is assigned a **Shininess** map.
Column 9: **I** if the material is assigned a **Self Illuminated** map.
Column 10: **R** if the material is assigned a **Reflection** map.
Column 11: **2** if the material is assigned a **2-sided** map.
Column 12: **W** if the material is a **Wire** material.
Column 13: **F** if the material is a **Face map** material.

In any of the thirteen columns where the materials are not affected by the assignment of maps, then the column will be blank.

If a material has been assigned a map of any kind, the object to which that material is applied must have a mapping icon applied to the object, otherwise the material will not show when the scene including the object is rendered. In general the mapping is applied with a **Planar** mapping icon. Despite the fact that the three glasses of the glasses scene are circular in plan, mapping was applied with the **Planar** icon. Fig. 2.22 shows a **Planar** mapping icon which has been adjusted to enable materials which have been assigned maps to be applied to each of the three glasses.

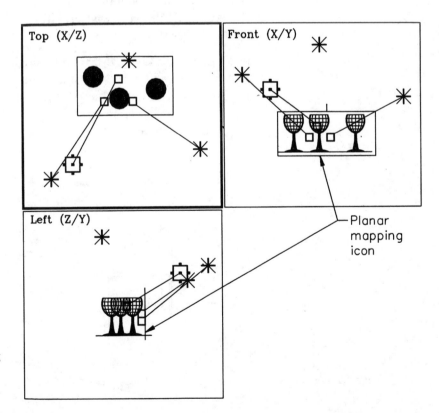

Fig. 2.22 A **Planar** mapping icon adjusted the three glasses of the three glasses scene

Background to a rendered scene

Fig. 2.23 Shows the dialogue box for selecting a background to be included with a scene.

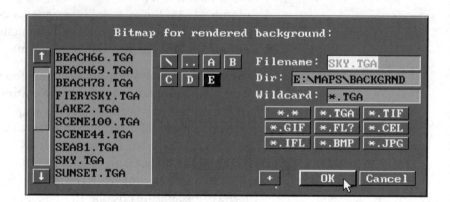

Fig. 2.23 The **Bitmap for rendered background** dialogue box

Two further examples of rendered DXF files

First example – a table

Fig. 2.24 is a 3D model drawing of a table, constructed in AutoCAD. The AutoCAD drawing was saved as a DXF file and loaded into 3D Studio. It was then rendered after:

1. The materials **WOOD MED.ASH** and **SAND TEXTURE** were added.
2. A background **GRAVEL1.CEL** was included.
3. Lights were added to the scene in a manner similar to those added to the three glasses scene.
4. A camera was added.

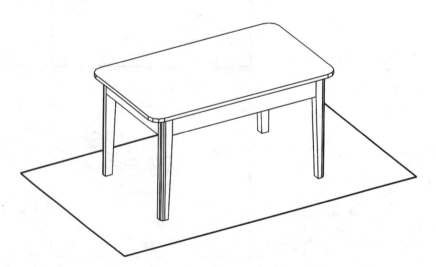

Fig. 2.24 An AutoCAD drawing of a 3D model of a table

Note: In this example, care had to be taken to ensure that the table top, leg and each rail were drawn as separate entities and, when in 3D Studio, the mapping icon was placed in suitable positions to make certain the applied wood grain was running in a correct direction on each item of the table.

Second example – an engineering component

Fig. 2.25 is a 3D model drawing of an assembly of an engineering feature constructed in AutoCAD. The AutoCAD drawing was saved as a DXF file, then loaded into 3D Studio. It was rendered after:

1. The materials **BLUE METALLIC**, **BRASS GIFMAP**, **CHROME GIFMAP** and **COPPER** were applied.
2. A background **WHITEASH.GIF** was included.
3. Lights and a camera were added in positions similar to those for the three glasses scene.

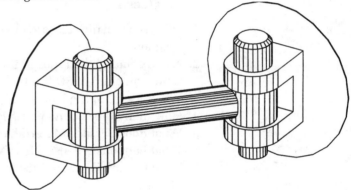

Fig. 2.25 An AutoCAD drawing of an engineering assembly

Filename extensions

A number of files, with a variety of filename extensions, are used in 3D Studio. Among those used in the **3D Editor** are the following:

*.dxf: Drawing files saved in DXF format. Can be loaded into the **3D Editor**.

*.flm: Filmroll files saved in AutoCAD. Can be loaded into the **3D Editor**.

*.3ds: Mesh files saved in 3D Studio in binary format. Can also be loaded into **3D Editor**.

*.asc: Mesh files saved in the **3D Editor** in ASCII format. Can also be loaded into the **3D Editor**.

*.tga: Rendered files are saved in this format. A bitmap format file.

*.tif: Can be used as Bitmap pictures.

*.gif: Bitmap pictures.

*.cel: Files produced by Autodesk Animator for mapping.

More information about extensions is given in Appendix B.

Notes

1. Filmroll files (those ending with the extension *.flm) can be loaded into the **3D Editor** in a manner similar to that for loading *.dxf files.
2. When applying material which are tiles, mapping may have to have tiling parameters adjusted in X and Y directions. **Surface/Mapping.../Adjust.../Tile** brings the **Map Tiling Setup** dialogue box on screen for this purpose.
3. If **Anti-aliasing** is set, the edges of the features in a scene will be slightly blurred.
4. **Phong** shading and anti-aliasing will require more time to render than the other forms of shading or no anti-aliasing.

Questions

1. What types of file can be loaded into 3D Studio from CAD software programs?
2. Name some of the types of files which can be used with the **3D Editor** program of 3D Studio.
3. What is a mapping icon?
4. How many types of mapping icon are there?
5. What does **Surface/Material.../Choose** mean?
6. What happens when **Surface/Materials.../Choose** is entered?
7. What type of file is produced when a 3D model is rendered in 3D Studio?
8. What is a Light **Falloff** cone in 3D Studio?
9. Why must some materials be mapped onto objects in a scene in the **3D Editor**?
10. How would you add a background scene into a 3D model to be rendered in the **3D Editor**?

Exercises

In order to allow the reader the opportunity of practising rendering of simple 3D models imported into 3D Studio from CAD software, these exercises will be simple 3D models constructed in AutoCAD, some with the aid of the Advanced Modelling Extension (AME). The models are to be constructed in AutoCAD (or other 3D CAD), saved as DXF files, and loaded into the **3D Editor**.

1. The pulley drawing of Fig. 2.26 was constructed from plines as shown. The holes in the pulley wheel are SOLCYLs which have

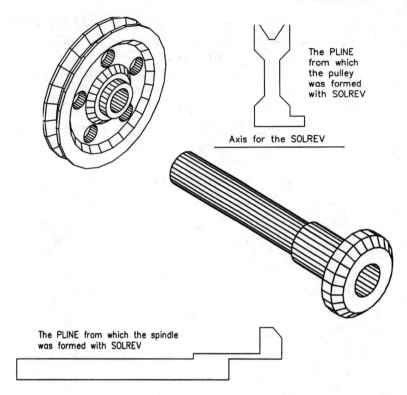

The PLINE from which the pulley was formed with SOLREV

Axis for the SOLREV

The PLINE from which the spindle was formed with SOLREV

Fig. 2.26 Exercises 1 and 2

been SOLSUBed from the wheel. In the **3D Editor** render the pulley wheel with a suitable metallic material and with a sand or granite type background.

2. The spindle to fit in the pulley (Fig. 2.26) was constructed as shown. Render the spindle with a different metallic material to that for the pulley. Go back to AutoCAD and fit the spindle into its hole

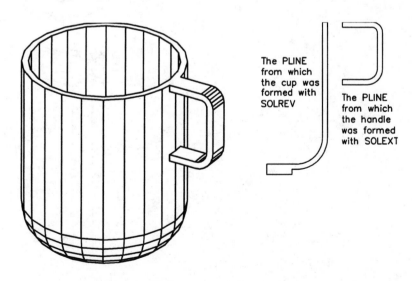

The PLINE from which the cup was formed with SOLREV

The PLINE from which the handle was formed with SOLEXT

Fig. 2.27 Exercise 3

in the pulley. Save as a DXF file, load into the **3D Editor** and render the combined model using two different metallic finishes – e.g. CHROME GIF and BLUE METALLIC.

3. The cup with its handle were constructed in AutoCAD as indicated in Fig. 2.27. They were then joined to each other with SOLUNION. The resulting 3D model can then be imported as a DXF file into the **3D Editor** and rendered with a suitable material. Try mapping the material onto the surface of the cup using a Cylindrical mapping icon.

4. Fig. 2.28. The model was constructed in AutoCAD with the aid of AME (Advanced Modelling Extension). Each part of the model was

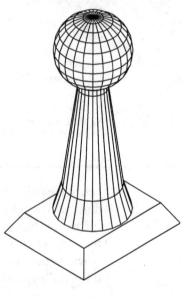

Fig. 2.28 Exercise 4

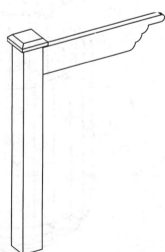

Fig. 2.29 Exercise 5

constructed on a different layer. Save as a DXF file and load into the **3D Editor**. Render in three different materials with a cloud background.

5. The 3D model of a finger post (Fig. 2.29) was constructed on three layers. Render in the **3D Editor** with a wood material, remembering that the grain of each part runs in a different direction requiring moving and/or rotating the Planar mapping icon on each part. Render in a suitable scenic background.

CHAPTER 3

Creating models in 3D Editor

Introduction

Examples of 3D models constructed in the **3D Editor** will be described in this chapter. A *left-click* on **Create** in the **3D Editor** command causes the names of the types of primitive solids from which 3D models can be constructed to appear in the command column – Fig. 3.1. The primitives can be acted upon by the three Boolean operators – Union, Subtract and Intersect (added to, subtracted from or intersected with each other) – to form the final required 3D model. When the model has been created lights, cameras, materials, mapping and backgrounds can be added to form a scene which includes the model. The scene can then be rendered.

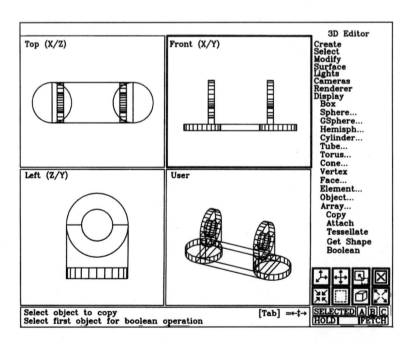

Fig. 3.1 The partly completed 3D model Example 1 created in the **3D Editor**

The primitive solids

As can be seen in the list of commands shown in Fig. 3.1, the following primitive solids can be created – **Box**, **LSphere**, **GSphere**, **Hemisphere**, **Cylinder**, **Tube**, **Torus** and **Cone**.

Box

1. *Left-click* in the viewport in which the box is to be created.
2. **Create/Box.**
3. Prompts:

   Place one corner of box. *Left-click* at the required position.
   Place opposite corner of box. *Left-click* at the required position.
   Check in viewport to define length of box. Move the mouse in **ANY** viewport, and the length of the box shows in the Status Line.

4. Dialogue box appears – **Name for new object** with a name such as **Object01** – Fig. 3.2. Enter another name if desired. *Left-click* on **Create** in the dialogue box.
5. The **Box** appears in all viewports.

Fig. 3.2 The **Name for new object** dialogue box

LSphere

1. *Left-click* in the viewport in which you are to create the LSphere.
2. **Create/LSphere.../Values.**
3. Dialogue box **Set Lat-Long Sphere Segments** – Fig. 3.3. Set the number required by moving the slider with the mouse to – say 16. *Left-click* on **OK**.
4. **Create/LSphere.../Smoothed.**
5. Prompts:

   Place centre of 16-segment smoothed LSphere.
   Set radius. Move the mouse in **ANY** viewport, and the radius of the sphere shows in the Status Line.

6. **Name for new object** dialogue box appears on screen. *Left-click* on **Create**.

Fig. 3.3 The **Set Lat-Long Sphere Segments** dialogue box

Note: If a faceted LSphere (or GSphere) is created the facets show when the object is rendered, even if rendering is **Phong** and anti-aliasing is **On**. When a smoothed Sphere is created a smooth outline will show when the sphere is rendered.

GSphere

1. *Left-click* in the viewport in which the GSphere is to be created
2. **Create/GSphere.../Values**.
3. Dialogue box **Geodesic Sphere Faces** – Fig. 3.4. Set number of faces as required – say 256. *Left-click* on **OK**.

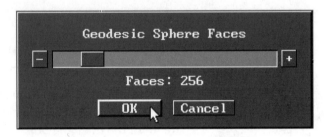

Fig. 3.4 The **Geodesic Sphere Faces** dialogue box

4. **Create/GSphere.../Smoothed**.
5. Prompts:

   Place centre of 256 face geodesic sphere.
   Set radius. Move the mouse in **ANY** viewport, and the radius of the sphere shows in the Status Line.

6. **Name for new object.** *Left-click* on **Create**.

Hemisphere

1. *Left-click* in the viewport in which the Hemisphere is to be created.
2. **Create/Hemisph.../Values**. Dialogue box **Set Hemisphere Segments**. Set a number – say 16 segments. *Left-click* on **OK**.
3. **Create/Hemisph.../Smoothed**.
4. Prompts:

   Place center of 16-segment smoothed hemisphere.
   Set radius. Move the mouse in **ANY** viewport, and the radius of the hemisphere shows in the Status Line.

5. **Name for new object.** *Left-click* on **Create**.

Cylinder

1. *Left-click* in·the viewport in which the Cylinder is to be created.
2. **Create/Cylinder.../Values**.

3. Dialogue box **Set Cylinder Values** appears on screen – Fig. 3.5. Set sides to say 24. Set segments to 1. *Left-click* on **OK**.

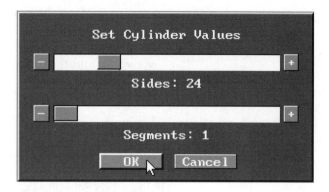

Fig. 3.5 The **Set Cylinder Values** dialogue box

4. **Create/Cylinder.../Smoothed**.
5. Prompts

Place center of 24-side, 1-segment smoothed cylinder.
Set radius. Move the mouse in **ANY** viewport, and the radius of the cylinder shows in the Status Line.
Check in viewport to define length of cylinder. Move the mouse in **ANY** viewport, and the length of the cylinder shows in the Status Line.

Tube

1. *Left-click* in the viewport in which the Tube is to be created.
2. **Create/Tube.../Values**.
3. Dialogue box **Set Tube Values** appears on screen – Fig. 3.6. Set sides to say 24. Set segments to say 1. *Left-click* on **OK**.

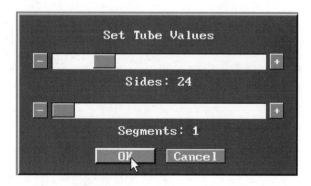

Fig. 3.6 The **Set Tube Values** dialogue box

4. **Create/Tube.../Smoothed**.
5. Prompts:

Place center of 24-side, 1-segment smoothed tube

Set radius 1. Move the mouse in **ANY** viewport, and the first radius for the tube shows in the Status Line.

Set radius 2. Move the mouse in **ANY** viewport, and the second radius for the tube shows in the Status Line.

Click in viewport to define length of tube. Move the mouse in **ANY** viewport, and the length of the tube shows in the Status Line.

6. **Name for new object.** *Left-click* on **Create**.

Cone

1. *Left-click* in the viewport in which the Cone is to be created.
2. **Create/Cone.../Values.**
3. Dialogue box **Set Cone Values**. Set Sides to say 16. *Left-click* on **OK**.
4. Prompts:

Place center of 16-side smoothed cone.

Set radius 1. Move the mouse in **ANY** viewport, and the radius of the bottom face of the cone shows in the Status Line.

Set radius 2. Move the mouse in **ANY** viewport, and the radius of the upper face of the cone shows in the Status Line.

Click in viewport to define length of cone. Move the mouse in **ANY** viewport, and the cone length shows in the Status Line.

5. **Name for new object.** *Left-click* on **Create**.

Array

1. *Left-click* in the viewport in which the Array is to be created. In the viewport **Create** say a cylinder.

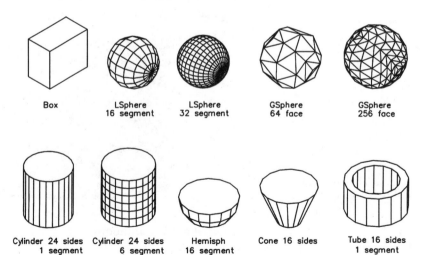

Box   LSphere 16 segment   LSphere 32 segment   GSphere 64 face   GSphere 256 face

Cylinder 24 sides 1 segment   Cylinder 24 sides 6 segment   Hemisph 16 segment   Cone 16 sides   Tube 16 sides 1 segment

Fig. 3.7 Some of the primitive solids which can be created in the **3D Editor**

2. **Create/Array.../Radial**.

3. Prompts:

> **Click on object to array radially** *left-click* on the cylinder.
> **Radial Array** dialogue box appears – Fig. 3.8. *Enter* 6 in the
> **Total number in array** box. *Enter* 60 in the **Degrees** box. *Left-click* on **Calculate** and the **Arc Length** figure adjusts automatically. The array appears in all viewports centred at coordinate
> 0,0,0.

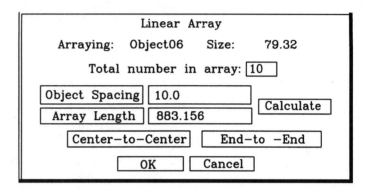

Fig. 3.8 The **Radial Array** dialogue box

4. Note the type of cursor associated with **Create/Array.../Linear** – Fig. 3.9.

5. With **Create/Array.../Linear**, a uni-directional cursor appears – Fig. 3.9. Pressing the **Tab** key changes its direction – up, down, left or right – to ensure the array is in the direction desired.

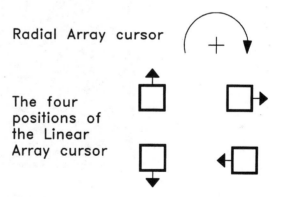

Fig. 3.9 The cursors associated with the **Create/Array...** commands

6. The **Linear Array** dialogue box is shown in Fig. 3.10.

First example – an engineering assembly

This model was constructed from a number of Boxes and Cylinders. Stages in the construction of the model are shown in pictorial form in

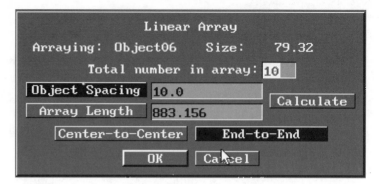

Fig. 3.10 The **Linear Array**
dialogue box

Fig. 3.12. The completed solid is shown in Fig. 3.13. The sequence
followed in the construction was.

1. *Left-click* on **View** and in the **View** pull-down menu, *left-click* on
   Drawing Aids. Set **Grid** and **Snap** as required.
2. Stage 1: **Create/Box** – construct three boxes of suitable sizes.
3. **Modify/Object.../Move** – move the two vertical boxes to a suitable
   position relative to the base box.
4. **Create/Object.../Boolean – Union** the three boxes. The **Boolean
   Operation** dialogue box appears – Fig. 3.11 – after selecting each
   pair of the boxes to be joined together. Prompts appear at the
   Prompt Line to assist the operator. Take care that the **Union** box
   is highlighted by a *left-click* in its outline.

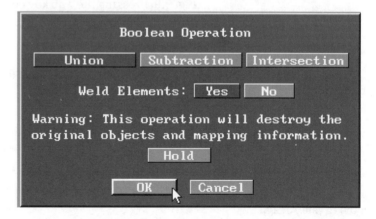

Fig. 3.11 The **Boolean
Operation** dialogue box

5. Stage 2: **Create/Cylinder.../Values**. Set the number of **Sides:** to 24
   in the **Set Cylinder Values** dialogue box which appears.
6. **Create/Cylinder.../Smoothed**. Create one cylinder and **Create/
   Object.../Copy** it to form a second cylinder. **Modify/Object.../Move
   the** cylinders to suitable positions.
7. Stage 3: **Create/Object.../Boolean**. **Subtract** each of the cylinders
   from the upright boxes in turn.

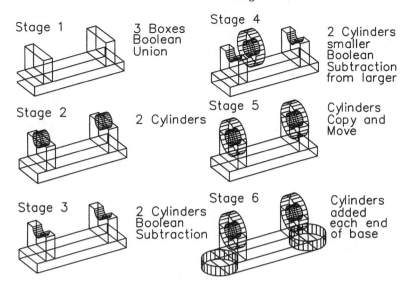

Fig. 3.12 The stages of
construction for Example 1

8. Stage 4: **Create/Cylinders.../Smoothed**. Create two cylinders, one
    for the outer, the second for the hole in the first. **Create/Object.../
    Boolean** and **Subtract** the smaller cylinder from the larger.
9. Stage 5: **Create/Object.../Copy**, followed by **Modify/Object.../
    Move** to place the two cylinders with their holes in position at top
    of the two upright boxes.
10. Stage 6: **Create/Cylinder.../Smoothed**. Create a cylinder, **Create/
    Object.../Copy**, followed by **Modify/Object.../Move** to position a
    cylinder at each end of the base.

The 3D model has now been constructed – Fig. 3.13 – and is ready
to have lights etc. included in a scene. These were:

Materials – Base: CHROME GIFMAP; **Spindle:** BRASS GIFMAP;
Pulley: CYAN METALLIC.
Background: TEXTUR01.TGA from the directory Samples/maps/
patterns in the CD-ROM supplied with 3D Studio Release 2.

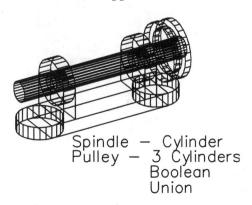

Spindle – Cylinder
Pulley – 3 Cylinders
Boolean
Union

Fig. 3.13 The completed 3D
model of the first example

Part 1
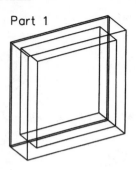

Part 2
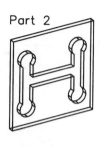

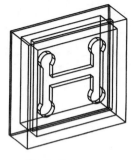

Inner Box: Boolean
Subtraction
from outer Box.
Rear Box added

4 Cylinders and
3 Boxes Boolean
Union together
and Boolean
subtraction from
outer Box

Part 2:
Boolean Union
with Part 1

Fig. 3.14 The first stages in
constructing the 3D model
for the second example

Lights: Ambient; Omni; 2 Spots.
Rendering: Phong; anti-aliasing On; Background: Rescaled.

Note: No attempt has been made to **Boolean Union** the cylinders to the
tops of the upright boxes or to the ends of the base.

Second example – a four-way wall switch

Figures 3.14 and 3.15 show the stages in the construction of this
example. The unit dimensions of the model do not really matter for the
purpose of this example.

Materials and background: When the 3D model had been constructed
in the **3D Editor** materials, mapping and a background were added
as follows:

Materials: BLACK PLASTIC (back); BRASS GIFMAP (handle rod);

Part 3
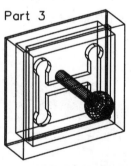

Final model
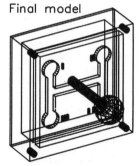

Fig. 3.15 The final stages in
constructing the 3D model
for the second example

Handle created
from Cylinder
and LSphere

Cylinders: Boolean
Subtraction from
Part 3. Figures and
Boxes added

CHROME GIFMAP (body); RED GLASS (handle knob); DEFAULT (numbers).

Background: WEAVE001.TGA from samples/maps/patterns on the CD-ROM.

Third example – a wall and window

Fig. 3.16 shows the stages in constructing the third example.

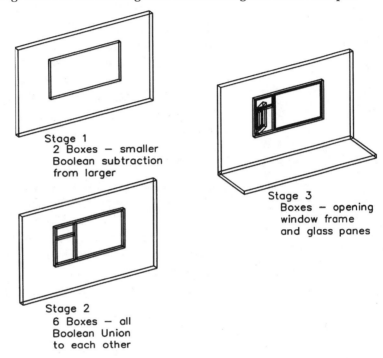

Stage 1
2 Boxes – smaller
Boolean subtraction
from larger

Stage 3
Boxes – opening
window frame
and glass panes

Stage 2
6 Boxes – all
Boolean Union
to each other

Fig. 3.16 The stages in constructing the 3D model for the third example

1. *Left-click* on **View** and in the **View** pull-down menu, *left-click* on **Drawing Aids**. Set **Grid** to 9 and **Snap** to 3.
2. *Left-click* in the **Front (X/Y)** viewport to make it active.
3. *Left-click* on the full screen icon in the **icon panel**. The **Front** viewport becomes the only viewport. All construction for the 3D model can be carried out in this single viewport.
4. Stage 1: **Create/Box** – create two boxes, each 9 units long, and **Boolean** subtract the smaller from the larger.
5. Stage 2: **Create/Box** – create the window frame and its bars from 6 boxes, each 6 units wide and 6 units long. **Boolean** union the 6 boxes together. Add a seventh box for the window sash making the smaller window.
6. Stage 3: **Create/Box** – create a window frame from four boxes 6 wide and 6 long; **Create/Box** – create the glass for each of the

required three spaces, making each box no more than 1 unit long. **Snap** must be turned off for this – *enter* an s at the keyboard; *Left-click* in the full screen icon to bring back all four viewports; In the **Top (X/Z)** viewport with the aid of the commands **Modify/Object.../Move** move the boxes of the 3D model to their required positions – window frames and glass. With the aid of **Modify/Object.../Rotate** rotate the window frame to an open position.

7. **Create/Box** – in the **Top (X/Z)** viewport, create a box for the floor 9 units long.

8. *Left-click* in the **Left (Z/Y)** viewport to make it active; **Modify/Object.../Move** and move the floor to its required position.

9. Add the following materials and a background:
    Materials: BROWN BUMPYBRICK (wall); WHITE PAINT (window frames); GLASS (glass); WOOD-WHITE ASH (floor).
    Background: COUDIV.TGA from the samples/maps/clouds directory of the CD-ROM supplied with 3D Studio release 2.

Notes

1. The term *long* used in this example refers to the length of the boxes as they are created in the viewport. In fact the lengths are really the depths from front to back of the window frame and its bar members.

2. Do not **Boolean** union the glass to its frames, the window frames to the wall nor the floor to the wall. Each of these parts (objects) is to be given a different material. If they were **Boolean** unioned, they could not be treated as objects requiring different material treatment.

Modify commands

It will have been noted that in constructing the 3D model for the third example above, two **Modify** commands were used – **Modify/Object.../Move** and **Modify/Object.../Rotate**. Solids created in the **3D Editor** can have their positions, angles and shapes modified with the aid of the **Modify** commands. Remember if you use these commands, any modification will apply to the whole of the selected solid, whether it is a primitive, or a solid created by the action of any of the **Boolean** operators. The **Modify** command set is:

Modify/Object.../Move
Modify/Object.../Rotate
Modify/Object.../2D Scale
Modify/Object.../3D Scale
Modify/Object.../Skew
Modify/Object.../Mirror

Modify/Object.../Bend
Modify/Object.../Taper
Modify/Object.../Align
Modify/Object.../Attributes
Modify/Object.../Reset Xform
Modify/Object.../Change Color
Modify/Object.../Get Color
Modify/Object.../Delete

When any one of the **Modify** commands is called, a unidirectional cursor in the form of a square with a pointing arrow appears in the selected viewport – see Fig. 1.20 page 13. The arrow will change direction from up/right to down/left as the **Tab** key of the keyboard is repeatedly pressed, indicating the direction in which the modification will take place.

Some examples of primitive solids created in the **3D Editor** and acted upon by the **Modify** commands are given in Fig. 3.17.

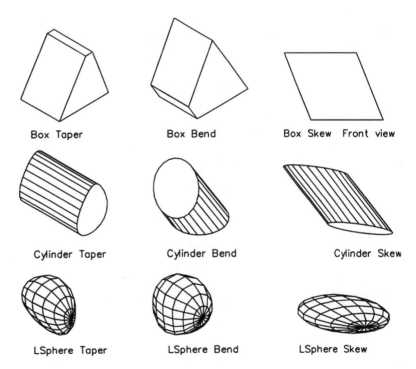

Box Taper   Box Bend   Box Skew Front view

Cylinder Taper   Cylinder Bend   Cylinder Skew

LSphere Taper   LSphere Bend   LSphere Skew

Fig. 3.17 Some examples of using the **Modify** commands on primitive solids

The HOLD and FETCH buttons

Below the icons in the **icon panel** (Fig.3.18) in the **3D Editor**, are two buttons labelled **HOLD** and **FETCH**. One of the problems of working in the **3D Editor** is that, if an error is made while creating a 3D model,

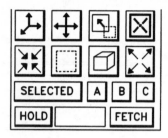

Fig. 3.18 The Icon panel of
the **3D Editor**

there is no method by which the error can be undone. Note that this does not apply to the other programs in 3D Studio. This problem can be overcome by using the **HOLD** and **FETCH** buttons. A *left-click* on the **HOLD** button saves what has been created in the **3D Editor**, the contents of the viewports being saved to a buffer. Once the **HOLD** button has been selected, further constructions in the viewports will be lost with a *left-click* on the **FETCH** button. This is because the **FETCH** button recalls the construction saved in the **HOLD** buffer and rejects all other work. Fig. 3.19 shows what happens when the two buttons are used. In Fig. 3.19:

Drawing 1: An LSphere is constructed with **Create/LSphere.../ Smoothed**. This is followed by a *left-click* on **HOLD**.
Drawing 2: The LSphere is skewed with **Modify/Object.../Skew**.
Drawing 3: The **FETCH** button is selected. The skewed LSphere disappears to be replaced by the original LSphere from the **HOLD** buffer.
Drawing 4: The LSphere is again acted on by **Modify/Object.../Skew**, followed by a *left-click* on the **HOLD** button.
Drawing 5: The modified LSphere is modified with **Modify/Object.../ Bend**.
Drawing 6: A *left-click* on **FETCH** brings back the skewed LSphere.

From these two examples of the use of **HOLD** and **FETCH**, it will be seen that if the **HOLD** button is selected each time one is satisfied with a construction to date, if an error then occurs, a *left-click* on **FETCH** brings back the satisfactory construction.

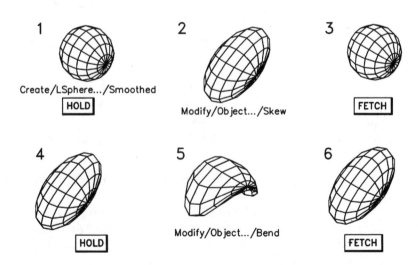

Fig. 3.19 The action of the
HOLD and **FETCH** buttons

3D Editor
Create
Select
Modify
Surface
Lights
Cameras
Renderer
Display
    Vertex...
    Face...
    Element
    Object...
    All
    None
    Invert
        Single
        Quad
        Fence
        Circle
        *Window
        Crossing
        By Name
        By Color

Fig. 3.20 The **Select** commands

Select commands

Left-click on **Select** in the **3D Editor** and the **Select** sub-menu appears in the command column – Fig. 3.20. *Left-click* on **Object...** in the menu and, in the selected viewport, *left-click* on selected objects. The selected objects change colour to red. In Fig. 3.21, the **Front (X/Y)** viewport has been changed to a single viewport, in which three of the objects – an LSphere, a Tube and a Torus – have been selected. As can be seen in Fig. 3.21:

All objects can be selected.

None can be selected.

Invert will deselect the selected objects and select the unselected ones.

Single will select a single object.

Quad allows a quadrilateral window within which a selection can be made.

Fence allows a 'fence' of as few or as many sides as required to surround objects for selection.

Circle allows selection within a circle.

Window will select all objects within the boundary of the window;

Crossing will select any object crossed by a window.

By Name bring on a dialogue box allowing selection of named objects.

By Color allows selection of those objects created by colour.

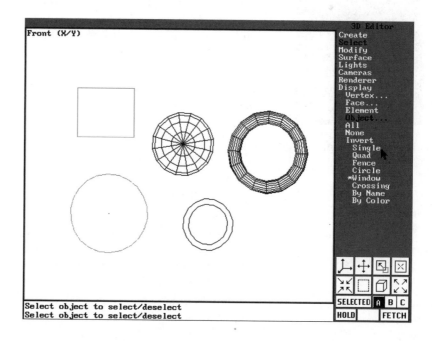

Fig. 3.21 An example of **Object** selection involving button **A**

Three buttons below the icon panel are labelled **A**, **B** and **C**. If a selection of objects is made and followed by a *left-click* on button **A**, the selected objects change to red. The selected objects will reappear as selected when the **A** button is again pressed. If button **B** is now selected, the selected objects in the viewport will revert to white. Further object selection will now be saved in buffer **B**. Similarly with button **C**. Thus three different groups of selections can be made with the aid of the three buttons. The **A**, **B** and **C** selections appear on screen when the appropriate button is selected. Fig. 3.21 shows the **A** selections.

Display commands

Left-click on **Display** in the **3D Editor** command list. As an example of the use of the **Display**, *left-click* on **Hide...**. At the lower end of the command column, a list of the features which can be hidden appears. This sequence is of particular value when one wishes to hide lights and cameras in order to carry on further work in viewports. As can be seen in Fig. 3.22 hidden features can be acted upon by **Unhide...** to bring them back in view. If an object is acted upon by **Freeze...**, the object highlights and cannot be acted upon by commands such as those in **Modify**, **Select** or **Surface**. For example one cannot **Assign** a surface to a frozen object or **Modify/Object.../Bend** the object. Whenever a frozen object is selected to be acted upon by any of these command sets, **No object found there** appears at the prompt line.

Note: No attempt is made here to give further explanation of the **Select** or **Display** commands. These are discussed later, together with more detail about the **Modify** commands. It is hoped, however, that sufficient detail has been given in this chapter to prompt the reader to experiment further with the creation of models in the **3D Editor**.

Fig. 3.22 The **Display** commands

Questions

1. What is the purpose of the **Hold** button in the **Icon panel**?
2. What happens when an object is selected by **Select/Object.../Single**?
3. How can a viewport be changed from showing a **Top** view to a **User** view?
4. An **LSphere** can be created with only **Lat-Long** segments. Why is it that a **Cylinder** can be constructed with both **Cylinder Values** and **Segments**?
5. What is the difference between an **LSphere** and a **GSphere**?

6. What does the **G** in **GSphere** stand for?
7. What is a **Boolean** operation?
8. How many types of **Boolean** operations can be performed on objects?
9. What is the purpose of the **Modify** commands?
10. How can one see that an object has been acted upon by **Display/Freeze.../Object**?

Exercises

1. Fig. 3.23. The sequence for constructing and rendering is:

(a)   **View/Drawing Aids** Set **Grid** to 20 in **X: Y:** and **Z:**
(b)   Enter **G** and **S** in each viewport to set Grid and Snap on.
(c)   **Create/Box** – 360 x 120 x 40.
(d)   **Create/Cylinder.../Smoothed** (16 sides).
(e)   **Create/Object.../Boolean** Union Box and Cylinder.
(f)   **Create/Cylinder.../Smoothed**.
(g)   **Create/Objects.../Boolean** Subtract last Cylinder from union.
(h)   **Create/Cylinder.../Smoothed** create the two holes.
(i)   **Create/Objects.../Boolean** Subtract the holes for the solid.
(j)   **G** and **S** in each viewport to turn **Grid** and **Snap** off.
(k)   Add an **Omni** and two **Spot** lights.
(l)   Add a **Camera**.
(m)   Add **Material** BRASS GIFMAP.
(n)   Add **Mapping.**
(o)   **Render**.

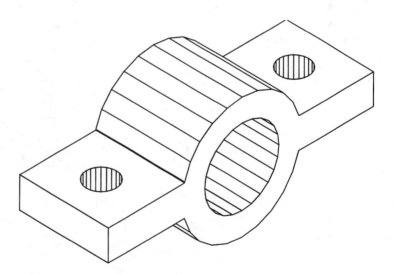

Fig. 3.23 Exercise 1

2. Fig. 3.24. The sequence for constructing and rendering is:

(a) **View/Drawing Aids** Set **Grid** to 20 in **X: Y:** and **Z:**
(b) Enter **G** and **S** in each viewport to set grid and Snap on.
(c) **Create/Cone.../Smoothed** Outer cone of glass.
(d) **Create/Cone.../Smoothed** Inner cone of glass.
(e) **Create/Object.../Boolean** Subtract inner cone from outer cone.
(f) **Create/Cone.../Smoothed** Stem.
(g) **Create/Cone.../Smoothed** Base.
(h) **Create/Object.../Boolean** Union base and stem.
(i) **Create/Object.../Boolean** Union base, stem and glass.
(j) **Create/Box** Create table top.
(k) **Surface/Materials.../Choose** BLUE GLASS.
(l) **Surface/Materials.../Apply** BLUE GLASS to wine glass.
(m) **Surface/Materials.../Choose** WOOD WHITE ASH.
(n) **Surface/Materials.../Apply** WOOD WHITE ASH to table top.
(o) **Surface/Mapping** Apply to both glass and table top.
(p) **Renderer/Background** TILE0003.TGA.
(l) **Renderer/Render** Render the Camera viewport.
     Shading: Phong.
     Anti-aliasing: On.
     Background: Rescale.

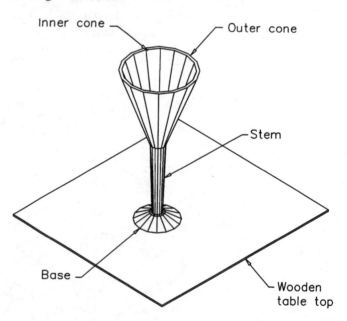

Fig. 3.24 Exercise 2

3. Figures 3.25 and 3.26. The methods of creating this 3D solid model are left to the reader's own judgement. The method of creating the corners for the box is given in Fig. 3.23. When the solid is created in the **3D Editor**, materials, mapping and rendering can be completed as follows:

Materials: Container - RED PLASTIC; Handle - WOOD WHITE ASH.

Surface/Mapping Apply only to the handle.

Renderer/Background TILE0009.TGA.

Renderer/Render Render the Camera viewport.

   Shading: Phong.

   Anti-aliasing: On.

   Background: Rescale.

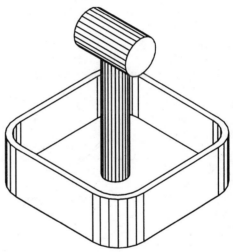

Fig. 3.25 Exercise 3

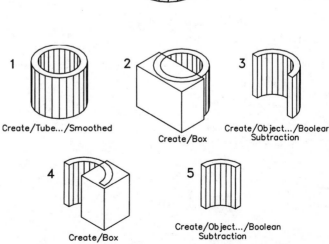

Fig. 3.26 Method of creating corners for Exercise 3

4. Fig. 3.27. A much simplified model of a domed building is given. Create the model to sizes of your own choice. Then add lights, camera, materials, mapping and rendering background:

Lights: Ambient, Omni and three Spot lights.
Camera: With 85 mm lens.
Materials: GOLD (dome); MARBLE GREEN (walls); CHROME GIFMAP (cross); BROWN MATTE (ground).
Background: CLOUD2.TGA from the CD-ROM sent out with the 3D Studio Release 2 software.
Render: Shading Phong; Anti-aliasing On; Background Rescaled.

Note: This last rendering took just under 3 minutes to complete, working with a 486DX2 machine. Working with a 386 might take up to 12 minutes.

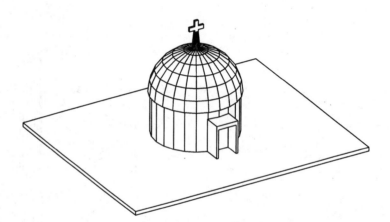

Fig. 3.27 Exercise 4

CHAPTER 4

Shapes

Introduction

Shapes are created in 3D Studio in the **2D Shaper** program. In the vocabulary of the software, a shape is a closed 2D polygon, the outline of which can be made up from lines, arcs, parts of ellipses etc. Text can also be treated as a shape.

To enter the **2D Shaper** program from the **3D Editor**, either:

1. *Left-click* on the name **3D Editor** at the top of the command column.
2. Or – *left-click* on **Program** in the **Menu bar**, followed by a *left-click* on **2D Shaper** in the **Program** pull-down menu (Fig. 4.1).
3. Or – press the **F1** key of the keyboard.

Whichever of these methods is followed the **2D Shaper** program screen appears. Note that this is normally a single viewport screen,

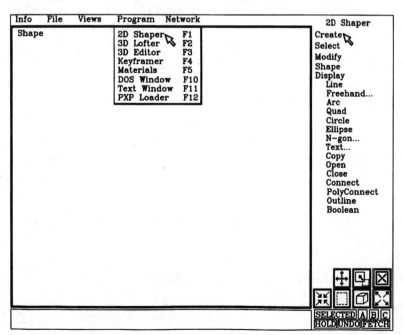

Fig. 4.1 The **2D Shaper** program screen with the **Program** pull-down menu

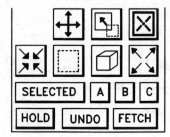

Fig. 4.2 The Icon panel of the **2D Shaper**

although it can be changed by a *left-click* on **Views** followed by a *left-click* on **Viewports** and then selecting the viewports layout required from the **Select the viewport division method** dialogue box which appears.

Only 2D shapes can be created in the **2D Shaper**. Because of this, the icon panel in the bottom right-hand corner is slightly different to that in the **3D Editor**. The first icon (top left) is missing. This icon allows the setting of the X,Y,Z axes in pictorial views in the viewport. Since only 2D shapes can be created in the **2D Shaper**, there is no requirement for this 3D facility. Otherwise the icon panel is the same as in the **3D Editor** – Fig. 4.2. Note that there is an **UNDO** button in the **2D Shaper** icon panel. This allows the last operation carried out to be undone.

Create

Left-click on **Create** in the **2D Shaper** command column – Fig. 4.1 – and the commands for creating 2D shapes appear. These are **Line**, **Freehand**, **Arc**, **Quad**, **Circle**, **N-gon**, **Text**. As any one of these is selected, with a *left-click*, prompts appear at the prompt line informing the operator of the steps to be taken to use the command. Figures 4.3 through to 4.9 show the outlines of the shapes, the prompts associated with the creation of each shape and some of the dialogue boxes and warning boxes involved with the shapes. Note that when creating any of the shapes, including text, vertices are included, showing as small crosses. It will be shown later (pages 59–61) that vertices play an important part in modifying both 2D shapes and 3D models.

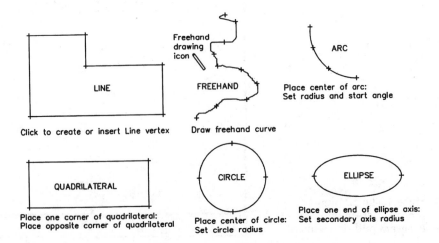

Fig. 4.3 Some outlines created in the **2D Shaper**, together with prompt line prompts

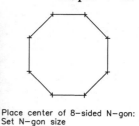

Fig. 4.4 The **Set N-Gon Sides** dialogue box

Place center of 8-sided N-gon:
Set N-gon size

Fig. 4.5 Some examples of fonts from 3D Studio

Text

Some examples of the variety of different types of font styles are shown in Fig. 4.5. To include text in a shape:

1. **Create/Text.../Font**: *left-click* on the name of the required font in the **Font File** dialogue box which appears – Fig. 4.6, followed by a *left-click* on **OK**.
2. **Create/Text.../Enter**: *Enter* the required text in the **Enter Text** dialogue box – Fig. 4.7.
3. **Create/Text.../Place**: *Left-click* following the prompts at the prompt line. The text appears in the box created by the two prompts – Fig. 4.8.

Note: If an attempt is made to place too much text on screen, the warning box Fig. 4.10 appears. At this stage, the reader is advised not to attempt changing the file **3DS.SET**, which is one of the files in the

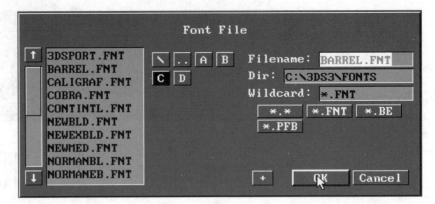

Fig. 4.6 Choosing a font from the **Font File** dialogue box

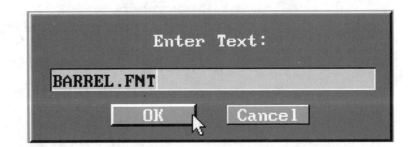

Fig. 4.7 The **Enter Text** dialogue box

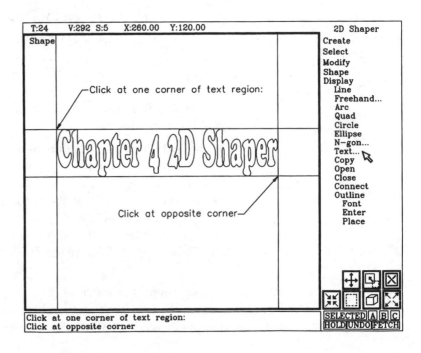

Fig. 4.8 Placing text following prompts at the prompt line

Text requires 240 vertices.
In use:480, Max:500. Use less
text, delete some vertices,
or change 3DS.SET.

OK

Fig. 4.9 The warning box
associated with too many
vertices when placing text

3D Studio software package and which controls features such as the
number of vertices allowed in a screen, the screen colours, etc.

Vertices and segments

When using the commands in **2D Shaper**, the prompt line includes
two names which recur in the use of 3D Studio – **vertices** and
segments. A **vertex** is shown on shapes with a small cross, a **segment**
is the line or curve between two vertices. All 2D shapes created in **2D
Shaper** depend upon these two features.

Other commands in Create

Seven other commands in the **Create** command list are **Create/Copy**,
Create/Open, **Create/Close**, **Create/Connect**, **Create/Poly-
Connect**, **Create/Outline** and **Create/Boolean**. Fig. 4.10 shows the
effects of using these commands. The illustration also includes the
prompts which appear at the prompt line.

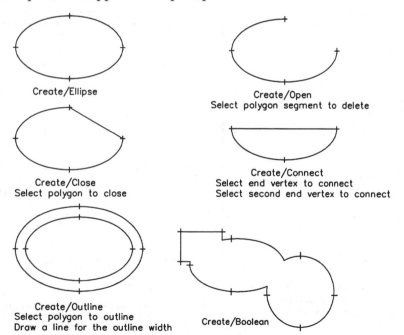

Create/Ellipse

Create/Open
Select polygon segment to delete

Create/Close
Select polygon to close

Create/Connect
Select end vertex to connect
Select second end vertex to connect

Create/Outline
Select polygon to outline
Draw a line for the outline width

Create/Boolean

Fig. 4.10 Other commands
in the **Create** command
column

Copy: (Not shown in Fig. 4.10.) **Create/Copy** brings a prompt into the prompt line to copy the whole polygon – the polygon being (in this case) an ellipse, which contains 4 vertices and the corresponding 4 segments.

Open: A *left-click* on any segment erases that segment.

Close: A *left-click* anywhere on an open polygon and a straight line joins the ends of the open polygon.

Connect: Two segments have been acted on by **Create/Open** in the ellipse; the two vertices of the open polygon can be closed with a straight line.

PolyConnect: Two open polygons can be connected to each other.

Outline: The polygon can be outlined with another similar polygon, the distance between the two polygons being determined by moving the mouse in the viewport.

Boolean: Boolean union, subtract or intersect shapes – compare with Boolean for objects in the **3D Editor** (page 42).

Fig. 4.11 shows another set of shapes which have been changed from a **Create/Line** outline with the use of the commands **Create/Open**, **Create/Close**, **Create/Connect** and **Create/Outline**.

Modify/Vertex...

Fig. 4.12 illustrates the use of some of the commands in the **Modify/**

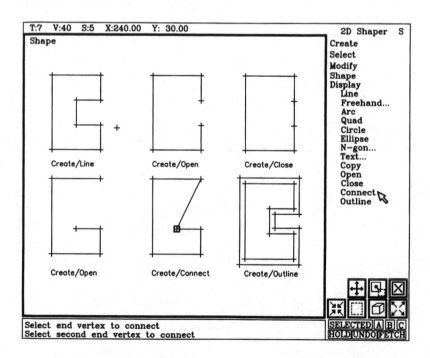

Fig. 4.11 Another example of the **Create** commands **Open, Close, Connect** and **Outline**

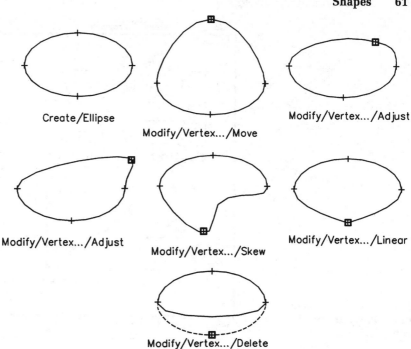

Fig. 4.12 Using the **Modify/
Vertex...** commands

Vertex... set. These commands can be used to greatly modify the outline of a shape in the **2D Shaper**. The set of commands can be used one after the other if it is thought necessary to modify any shape created in the viewport. When using these commands, prompts will appear in the prompt line instructing the operator how to use the commands. The modifications are always performed after selecting the vertex on which the modification is based and moving it as required. With some of the commands a pair of arrows of different colours shows the direction of the tangents of the spline curves beingformed in the modification.

Modify/Polygon...

Fig. 4.13 shows how a complete polygon can be changed in outline with the aid of the commands in **Modify/Polygon...**. In the **Polygon.../Adjust** example, the arrows indicating the direction of the adjustment taking place to form the curves are shown in the illustration. This particular polygon was drawn with **Create/Line**.

Again, the prompt line will show prompts advising the operator of what must be done to complete the action of any of the **Modify** commands.

A similar set of commands is available for modifying other polygons – **Arc**, **Circle**, etc.

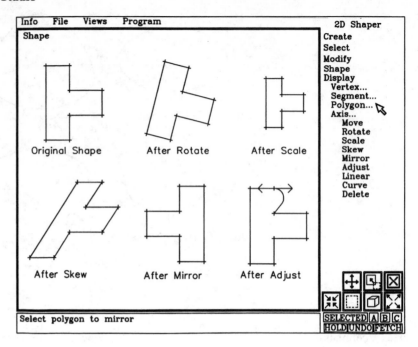

Fig. 4.13 The results of some of the **Polygon.../Modify** commands

Creating and transferring shapes

A shape created in the **2D Shaper** program can be transferred to the **3D Editor** or to the **3D Lofter** programs. Shapes are composed of a number of triangular surface meshes and are therefore the same type of feature as the surfaces of solids created in the **3D Editor**. A shape created in the **2D Shaper** can be transferred to the **3D Editor** with **Create/Object.../Get Shape**. Once in the **3D Editor** it can be rendered in the same way in which solid models are rendered. A shape can also be transferred to the **3D Lofter** program, in which it can be used as the surface from which a 3D solid model can be extruded and modified. The shape (Fig. 4.14) created in the **2D Shaper** can be transferred to other programs in 3D Studio using sequences such as the following:

In 2D Shaper

1. Create the shape – an example is given in Fig. 4.14, in which **Create/Line** and **Create/Arc** were called to create the shape.
2. **Shape/Assign** and assign the shape.

In 3D Editor

1. *Left-click* on **3D Editor** in the **View** pull-down menu.
2. **Create/Object.../Get Shape** – Fig. 4.15.
3. In the **Shape Creation Control** dialogue box, *left-click* on **OK**.
4. The shape appears in all four viewports – Fig. 4.16.
5. The shape can now be rendered if required.

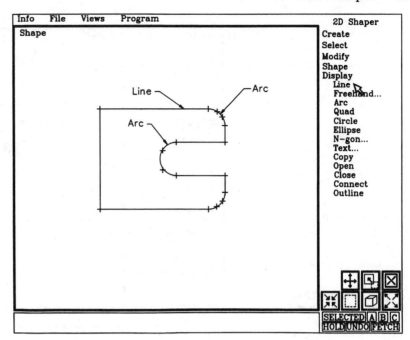

Fig. 4.14 Creating a shape in the **2D Shaper**

Fig. 4.15 **Create/Object.../Get Shape** in the **3D Editor**

Fig. 4.16 **Create/Object.../Get Shape** in the **3D Editor**

In 3D Lofter

1. *Left-click* on **3D Lofter** in the **program** pull-down menu.
2. **Shapes/Shaper** and the shape appears in all four viewports of the **3D Lofter** – (Fig. 4.18).

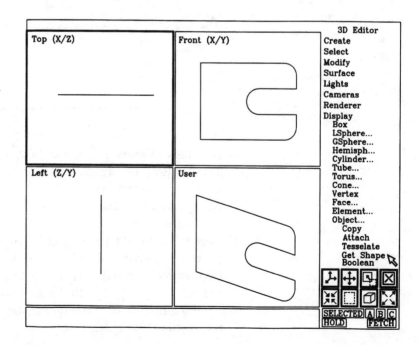

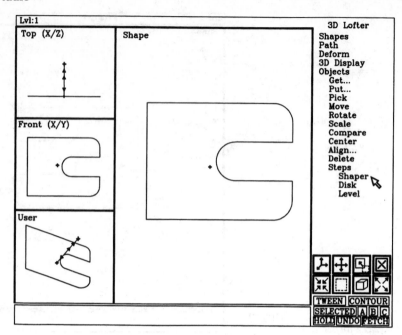

Fig. 4.17 **Shapes/Get.../**
Shaper to bring shape into
the **3D Lofter**

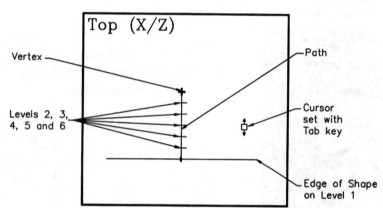

Fig. 4.18 The **Top (X/Z)**
viewport of the **3D Lofter**

3. **Path/Move Vertex.** In the **Top (X/Z)** viewport (Fig. 4.18) press the Tab key until the unidirectional cursor is pointing vertically up/down. Adjust the vertex in the **Top (X/Z)** viewport until it is 20 units above the shape. Figures in the Status bar will show the necessary units.

4. **Objects/Make** and the **Object Lofting Controls** dialogue box appears – Fig. 4.19. If satisfied with the settings *left-click* on **OK**.

5. **Objects/Preview** and the **preview Controls** dialogue box appears – Fig. 4.20. If satisfied with the settings *left-click* on **OK**.

6. The **3D Lofter** display changes to show a solid model appearing in its viewports – Fig. 4.21.

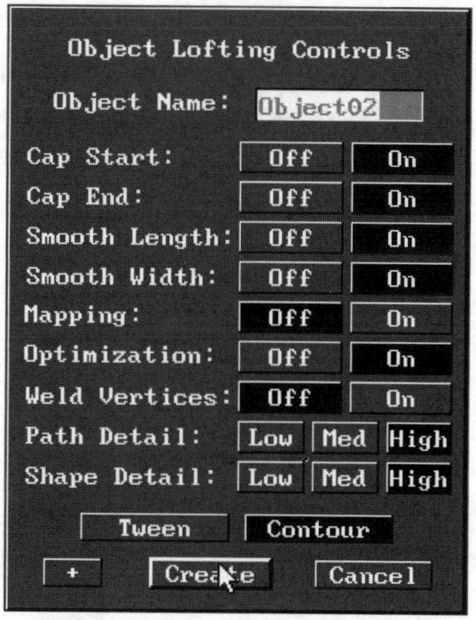

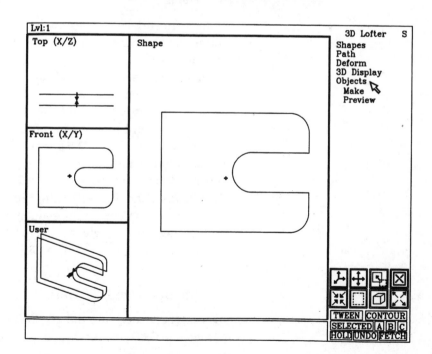

Fig. 4.19 The **Object Lofting Controls** dialogue box

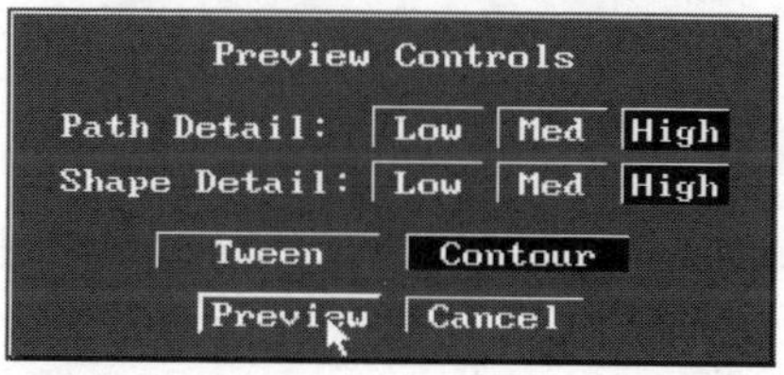

Fig. 4.20 The **Preview Controls** dialogue box

Fig. 4.21 The shape lofted 20 units in the **3D Lofter**

In 3D Editor

1. *Left-click* on **3D Editor** in the **View** pull-down menu.
2. The solid model from the **3D Lofter** appears in all four viewports of the **3D Editor** – Fig. 4.22.

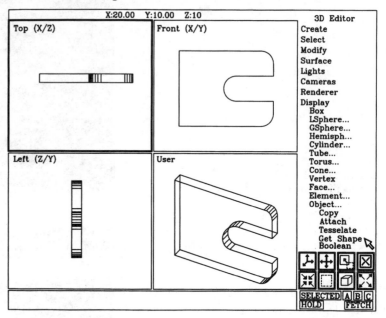

Fig. 4.22 The lofted shape in the **3D Editor**

Notes

1. Shapes are surface meshes made up from a number of triangular surface meshes, the vertices of the triangles being at the vertices of the shapes.
2. Shapes are useful in the **3D Editor**, even though they are 2D shapes. They can be used as surfaces in their own right or can be used as features such as backgrounds, walls, ceilings and floors of rooms.
3. A complete solid model can be assembled in this manner from shapes created in the **2D Shaper**, assigned and transferred with **Shapes/Shaper into** the 3D Lofter, lofted with **Objects/Make** and **Objects/Preview** along a **Path** and then acted upon by **Create/ Object.../Boolean** in the **3D Editor**. In this manner the shape shown in the three programs in the sequence above can be added to and then created into a single solid in the **3D Editor** ready for rendering – an example is given in Fig. 4.23.

Shapes from DXF files

Shapes can be loaded into the **2D Shaper** from DXF files of outlines constructed in CAD programs such as AutoCAD, AutoSketch, Generic

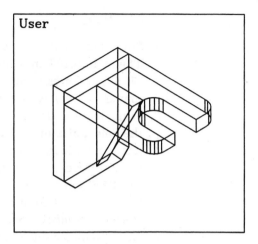

Fig. 4.23 Three shapes, lofted in the **3D Lofter** and created as a single 3D model in the **3D Editor**

CADD and other CAD programs supporting the DXF capability. Fig. 4.24 shows three examples. The solids were constructed in 3D Studio by:

1. Outlines were constructed in AutoCAD with the aid of the Pline command.
2. Each outline was saved as a DXF file.
3. Each DXF file was loaded into the **2D Shaper**.
4. **Shape/Assign/All** in the **2D Shaper** allowed the shapes to be transferred to the **3D Lofter** by **Shape/Get.../Shaper**.
5. The shapes were lofted in the **3D Lofter** by **Objects.../Make** and **Objects.../Preview**. In the example Shape 2, the object was made with **Tween** off and also with **Tween** on.

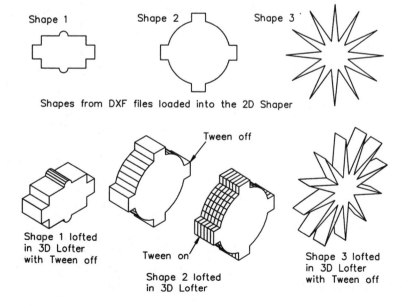

Fig. 4.24 Shapes from DXF files loaded into the **2D Shaper** and lofted in **3D Lofter**

Notes

1. Some shapes do not easily load from DXF file into the **2D Shaper**. The main problem is that the shape **MUST** be a closed polygon.
2. Circles and arcs from DXF files may not load easily because they may have too few vertices.
3. When loading DXF files make sure the ***.DXF** button is selected in the **Select 3DS or DXF file to load** dialogue box.
4. It is sometimes easier to construct an outline in a CAD package and use its DXF capability for loading shapes, than to create a shape in the **2D Shaper**.
5. Shapes loaded from DXF files can be modified with **Modify.../Vertex...**, **Modify.../Segment...** or **Modify.../Polygon...** in the same way in which a shape which has been created in the **2D Shaper** can be modified.

Exercises

1. Construct the model shown by Fig. 4.25. The 3D model was created by:

   (a) **2D Shaper: Create/Line**, followed by **Shape/Assign/All**.
   (b) **3D Lofter: Objects.../Make** and **Objects.../Preview** after the shape had been lofted.
   (c) **3D Editor:** User view.

2. Construct the model shown by Fig. 4.25. The 3D solid model was created by:

   (a) **D Shaper: Create/Freehand.../Draw** followed by **Shape/Assign\All**.

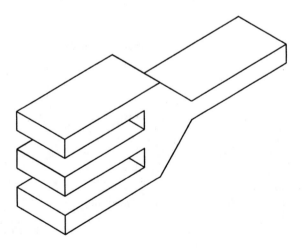

Fig. 4.25 Exercise 1

(b) **3D Lofter: Objects.../Make** and **Objects.../Preview** after the shape had been lofted.

(c) **3D Editor**: User view.

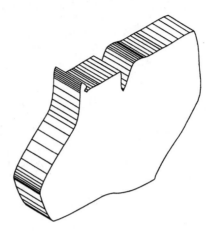

Fig. 4.26 Exercise 2

3. Construct the model shown by Fig. 4.27. The 3D solid model was created by:

(a) **2D Shaper: Create/Quad** followed by **Assign/All**.

(b) **3D Lofter: Objects.../Make** and **Objects.../Preview** after the shape had been lofted.

(c) **3D Editor**: User view.

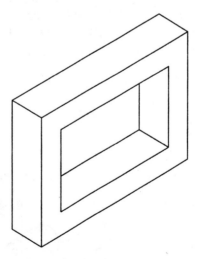

Fig. 4.27 Exercise 3

4. Construct the solid model shown by Fig. 4.28. The 3D solid model was created by:

(a) **2D Shaper: Create/Circle, Create/Ellipse** and **Create/Polygon**, followed by **Shape/Assign/All**.

(b) **3D Lofter Objects.../Make** and **Objects.../Preview** after the shape had been lofted.

(c) **3D Editor**: User view.

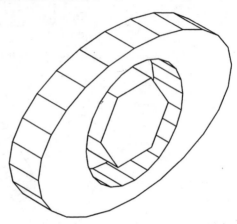

Fig. 4.28 Exercise 4

5. Construct the model shown in Fig. 4.29. The 3D solid model was created by:

(a) **2D Shaper**: **Create/Text.../Font, Create/Text.../Enter** and **Create/Text.../Place** using the **SERIFREG.FNT** followed by **Shape/Assign/All**.

(b) **3D Lofter**: **Objects.../Make** and **Objects.../Preview** after the shape had been lofted.

(c) **3D Editor**: User view.

(d) The 3D solid model was then assigned a material, lights and a camera and rendered.

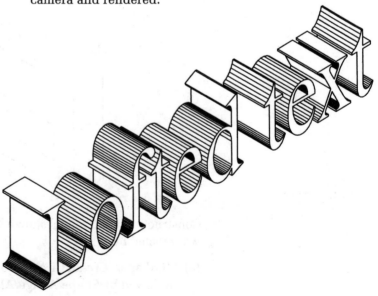

Fig. 4.29 Exercise 5

CHAPTER 5

The 3D Lofter program

Introduction

The **3D Lofter** has already been briefly referred to in Chapter 4. Further explanation of its functions is given in this chapter. To call the **3D Lofter** program, either *left-click* on **Program** in the menu bar, followed by a *left-click* on **3D Lofter** in the **Program** pull-down menu (Fig. 5.1) or press the **F2** key of the keyboard. The **3D Lofter** screen appears (Fig. 5.2). Another method of calling the **3D Lofter** program depends upon which of the four programs of 3D Studio has been previously used. For example, if working in the **2D Shaper**, a *left-click* on its name at the top of the command column will bring up the **3D Lofter**. A further *left-click* on the name **3D Lofter** in that program takes one back to the **2D Shaper**. If working with the **3D Editor** and the **3D Lofter**, *left-clicks* toggle between the two programs. If working in the **3D Editor** and the

Fig. 5.1 **3D Lofter** in the **Program** pull-down menu

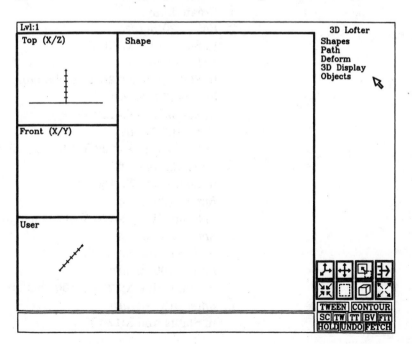

Fig. 5.2 The **3D Lofter** screen

Click to
switch
viewports

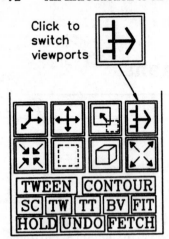

Fig. 5.3 The icon panel of
the **3D Lofter**

2D Shaper, *left-clicks* toggle between these two programs. The operator therefore has a choice between function key selection (**F1 – 2D Shaper, F2 – 3D Lofter, F3 – 3D Editor**), toggling with *left-clicks* or selection from the **Program** pull-down menu.

The 3D Lofter icon panel

As can be seen in Fig. 5.2, the icon panel is again different from those of the other two programs discussed in Chapters 1 to 4. The User view pictorial tripod is included, a new icon appears (switch viewports) and two buttons labelled **TWEEN** and **CONTOUR** appear. The use of these two buttons will be explained later. The icons in the panel have the same actions as those in the **3D Editor** and the **2D Shaper**. Five other buttons are included in the **3D Lofter** icon panel – labelled **SC** (SCale), **TW** (TWist), **TT** (TeeTer), **BV** (BeVel) and **FIT**. These buttons highlight when the **Deform** set of commands is in use – see later in this chapter. Note there is an **UNDO** in the panel. A *left-click* on this button undoes the last action taken – but only the last action. Two *left-clicks* on **UNDO** and the undone action is itself undone, thus reverting what was on the screen before the button was pressed.

Shapes created in the 2D Shaper

The shape from which the models in Fig. 5.7 were lofted could have been created in the following manner in **2D Shaper**:

1. **Create/Line**.
2. *Enter* 120 *Return*
   In Status line **X:120 Y:**
   Enter 60 *Return*
   In Status line **X:120 Y:60** changing to **X:**
3. *Enter* –120 *Return*
   In Status line **X:–120 Y:**
   Enter 100 *Return*
   In Status line **X:–120 Y:100** changing to **X:**
4. *Enter* 120 *Return*
   In Status line **X:–120 Y:**
   Enter –120 *Return*
   In Status line **X:–120 Y:–120** changing to **X:**
5. *Enter* 120 *Return*
   In Status line **X:120 Y:**
   Enter –100 *Return*
   In Status line **X:120 Y:–100** changing to **X:**
6. *Enter* –120 *Return*
   In Status line **X:120 Y:**

Enter –100 *Return*
In Status line **X:120 Y:–100**

7. *Enter* 120 *Return*
In Status line **X:120 Y:**
Enter –60 *Return*
In Status line **X:120 Y:–60**

8. Press the **Esc** key to come out of **Create/Line.**
9. **Create/Arc.**
10. *Left-click* on *X,Y* = 120,0.
11. *Left-click* on *X,Y* = 120,–60.
12. *Left-click* on *X,Y* = 120,60.

The dialogue box **Connect these vertices?** appears. *Left-click* on **Yes**.

Notes

1. If a mistake is made when entering a coordinate, press the **Esc** key of the keyboard and enter the correct coordinates. If a part of a polygon has been incorrectly entered **Modify/Polygon.../Delete** and delete the incorrect polygon and start again.
2. The same method of entering coordinates, but with different prompts appearing at the prompt line, can be employed when creating Circles, Arcs, Quads or N-gons.
3. In **3D Lofter Shapes/Get.../Shaper** brings any shapes created in the **2D Shaper** into the **Shape** viewport of the **3D Lofter**. An example is shown in Fig. 5.4. This shape can now be lofted into a 3D model by following the steps.

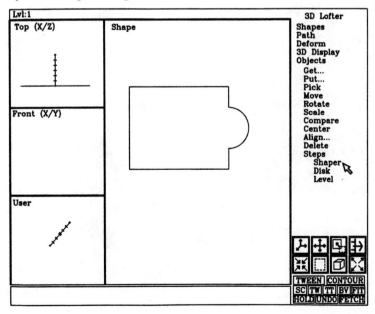

Fig. 5.4 A shape created in **2D Shaper** in **3D Lofter**

Fig. 5.5 The **Object Lofting Control** dialogue box

Fig. 5.6 The **Path** sub-set of commands in the **3D Lofter**

Fig. 5.7 Examples of **Path/Helix** and **Path/SurfRev**

4. **Path/Move Vertex** and move the vertex in the **Top (X/Z)** viewport to a suitable height.
5. **Objects/Make**. In the **Object Lofting Controls** dialogue box which appears (Fig. 5.5), note that the **Contour** button is highlighted and the **TWEEN** button is not highlighted. *Left-click* on **OK**.
6. Call the **3D Editor** and the lofted shape appears in all four viewports of that program.

Note: *Left-clicks* will now toggle between the **3D Lofter** and the **3D Editor** programs if necessary.

Path command set

The example just given dealt only with a 3D solid (Object) which had been lofted along a straight, vertical path after **Path/Move Vertex** has been applied to the path vertex to change its length. Other path shapes can be set by selection from the commands in the **Path** sub-set – Fig. 5.6. These allow a path to be set which is, for example, helical or circular. Two examples are given in Fig. 5.7 – a 3D model formed along a path set with **Path/Helix** and another formed along a path set with **Path/SurfRev**. The Shape from which the helical model and the revolved solids were formed is included in the figure, together with two simple vertically lofted models, one in which **TWEEN** was turned off and the other in which **TWEEN** was turned on from the **Object Lofting Controls** dialogue box.

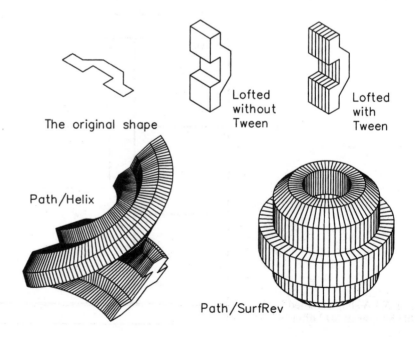

The original shape

Lofted without Tween

Lofted with Tween

Path/Helix

Path/SurfRev

When **Path/Helix** is selected a dialogue box **Helix Path Definition** (Fig. 5.8) allows the **Start Diameter** and the **End Diameter** to be set; the **Height** of the helix and the number of **Turns**. The helix can be made to form in a clockwise (**CW**) or counter clockwise (**CCW**) direction by a *left-click* on the appropriate button in the dialogue box.

When **Path/RevSurf** is selected, a dialogue box **Surface of Revolution** appears (Fig. 5.9), in which the **Diameter**, the number of **Degrees** required and the number of **Vertices** can be set.

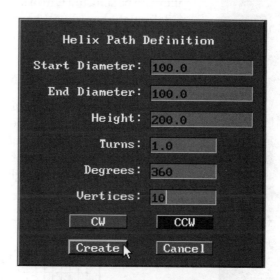

Fig. 5.8 The **Helix Path Definition** dialogue box

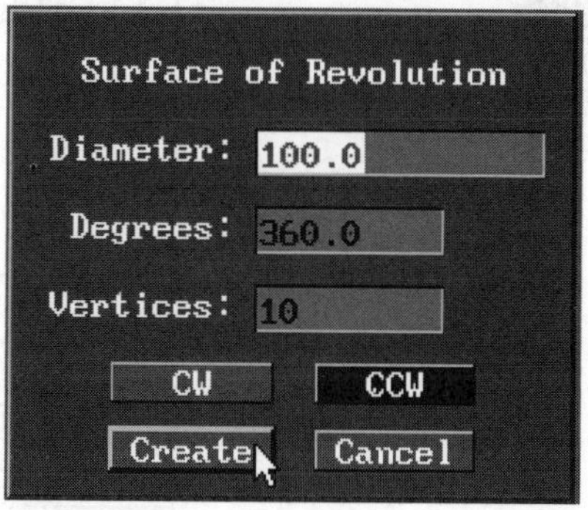

Fig. 5.9 The **Surface of Revolution** dialogue box

Deform command set

Left-click on **Path/Deform** and the Deform command set appears – Fig. 5.10. The **Path** can be 'deformed', with the aid of commands from this set – it can be scaled, twisted, teetered or bevelled as required. To assist the operator in determining the extent of the deformation, the **Scale**, **Twist**, **Teeter** and **Bevel** commands have deformation grids associated with the commands. These deformation grids appear in the **Shape**

viewport, the name of which changes to the **Deform** command name which has been selected. An example – of the **Bevel** deformation grid – is given in Fig. 5.11. The path in the deformation grids can have its position changed with **Move**, or have its shape altered with **Insert**. In the example shown in Fig. 5.11, the path line has been changed with the aid of **Insert**. When any of the **Deform** commands are applied to the path, the respective buttons among those marked **SC**, **TW** etc. in the icon panel will highlight in response to the use of the command. Or – they can be selected with a *left-click* and whatever **Scale**, **Twist** etc. has a deformation grid will be applied to the object when it is made and previewed with **Object/Make** and/or **Object/Preview**.

Deform with TWEEN off

Fig. 5.12 shows the results of lofting the shape shown in Fig. 5.4 after it has been acted upon by the commands in the **Deform** set – **Deform/Scale...**, **Deform/Twist...**, **Deform/Teeter...** and **Deform/Bevel....** The drawings in Fig. 5.12 are of the shape which has been lofted with **TWEEN** off – i.e. it is not highlighted. Thus only the outline of the 3D models is showing.

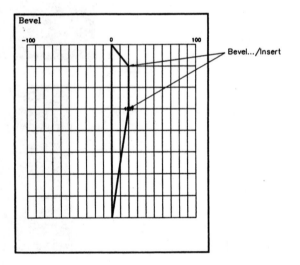

Fig. 5.10 The **Deform** deformation set grid

Deform with TWEEN on

In Fig. 5.13 examples of the action of the **Deform** set of commands with **TWEEN** on are shown. Taking the drawing labelled **Bevel** as an example, the model was created as follows:

1. A rectangular shape was created in the **2D Shaper** and placed in the **3D Lofter** with **Shape/Get.../Shaper**.

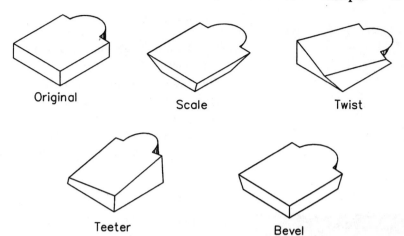

Fig. 5.12 A lofted shape acted upon by commands from the **Deform** command set with **TWEEN** off

2. **Path/Steps** brings up the **Set Path Steps** dialogue box. Adjust the slider to show **Steps: 8**.
3. **Deform.../Bevel...** and the **Shape** viewport changes to **Bevel** with the bevel deformation grid showing (Fig. 5.11).
4. **Deform/Bevel.../Insert** and move the Bevel line with the aid of the mouse and the unidirectional cursor. As the bevel line is moved, figures appear in the status line showing the position of the cursor – and the movement of the bevel line in units based upon those of the bevel deformation grid.
5. **Objects/Make**, followed by a *left-click* on **3D Editor** in the **Program** pull-down menu.
6. The 3D model appears in all four viewports of the **3D Editor**.

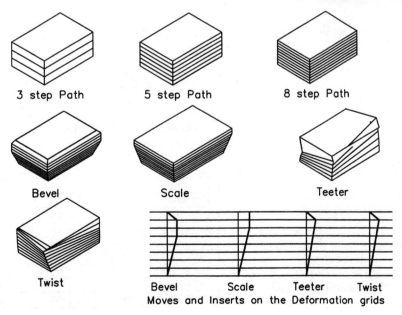

Fig. 5.13 The results of the action of **Deform** commands with **TWEEN** on

Notes

1. The 3D model bevels are based upon the path lines in the bevel deformation grid.
2. The other commands in the **Deform** set have similar deformation grids appearing in the **Shape** viewport when they are selected.
3. With each of the **Deform** commands guidance as to the deformations being performed on the grids are shown in unit sizes or angles in the Status bar above the viewport in which the grid appears.

Objects/Make

Fig. 5.14 The **Object Lofting Controls** dialogue box

A *left-click* on **Objects** followed by a *left-click* on **Make** brings up the **Objects Lofting Controls** dialogue box. This has already been shown in Fig. 5.5 as it appears in the **3D Lofter** screen. This is repeated in Fig. 5.14. A *left-click* on any one of the buttons in the dialogue box causes it to highlight (it turns red). Figures 5.15 and 5.16 show the results of setting the **On** or **Off** buttons in the dialogue box. It will be seen from the diagrams in these two figures that the object can be lofted to produce an outline only, an outline with tweening, an object with surface meshes at either one or both ends, an outline in which the Path and Shape details are low. In fact, by careful tuning of the various buttons in the dialogue box either on or off, the operator has complete control over the lofting process. The reader is advised to experiment with these settings. Note the **Make/Preview** command.

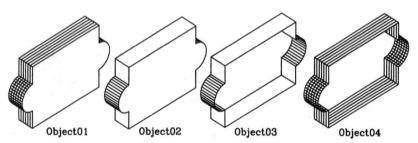

Fig. 5.15 Some examples of the results of different settings in the **Object Lofting Controls** dialogue box

	Object01	Object02	Object03	Object04
Cap Start	ON	ON	OFF	OFF
Cap End	ON	ON	OFF	OFF
Smooth Length	ON	ON	ON	OFF
Smooth Width	ON	ON	ON	ON
Optimisation	ON	ON	ON	ON
Path Details	HIGH	HIGH	HIGH	HIGH
Shape Detail	HIGH	HIGH	HIGH	HIGH
TWEEN	ON	OFF	OFF	ON
CONTOUR	ON	ON	ON	ON

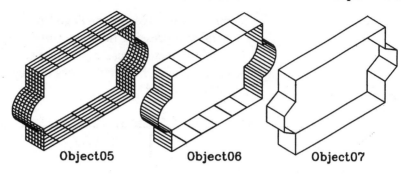

Object05   Object06   Object07

Fig. 5.16 Further examples
of the results of different
settings in the **Object
Lofting Controls** dialogue
box

	Object05	Object06	Object07
Cap Start	OFF	OFF	OFF
Cap End	OFF	OFF	OFF
Smooth Length	OFF	OFF	OFF
Smooth Width	OFF	OFF	OFF
Optimisation	OFF	OFF	OFF
Path Details	HIGH	LOW	LOW
Shape Detail	HIGH	HIGH	LOW
TWEEN	ON	OFF	OFF
CONTOUR	ON	ON	ON

This allows changes in the settings to be seen without having to toggle into the **3D Editor** program in order to see the results of any changes made in the **Object Lofting Controls** dialogue box.

Fig. 5.17 The **Set Path Steps**
dialogue box

Note: The number of steps for tweening can be set from **Path/Steps**. This brings up the **Set Path Steps** dialogue box – Fig. 5.17, in which the number of steps can be set by adjustment of the slider in the slider bar of the box, followed by a *left-click* on **OK**.

Path levels

In the Status Line of the **3D Lofter**, the abbreviation **Lvl:** followed by a number will be seen – Fig. 5.18. This shows the level at which the shape obtained from the **2D Shaper** has been placed. Levels can be

Lvl:4

Top (X/Z)   Shape

Fig. 5.18 **Lvl:** in the Status
Line of the **3D Lofter**

changed by pressing the **Page Up** key of the keyboard to move up one level and pressing the **Page Down** key to move the shape down one level. Repeated pressing of these two keys will move the shape to the desired level. Fig. 5.19 shows the levels when the **3D Lofter** program is first opened.

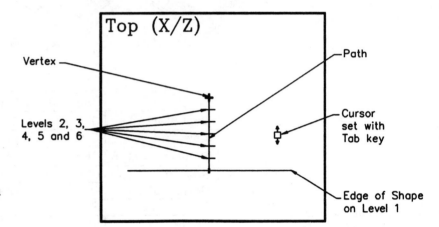

Fig. 5.19 The Path Levels in the **Top (X/Z)** viewport of the **3D Lofter**

Models with different shapes at different levels

Fig. 5.20 shows two examples of 3D models derived from Shapes at different levels lofted in the **3D Lofter**. The commands to create the left-hand model of the two shown, would follow a sequence such as:

1. In **2D Shaper**, create two (or more) shapes.
2. **Shape/Assign** *left-click* on largest shape. Its outline turns yellow.
3. In **3D Lofter, Shape/Get/Shaper**. Shape appears in the **Shape** viewport and at Level 1 in the **Top (X/Z)** viewport.
4. Press the **Page Up** key three times. Level 4 highlights in the **Top (X/Z)** viewport and the shape disappears from the **Shape** viewport.
5. In **2D Shaper, Shape/Assign/None** to release the shape already assigned.
6. **Shape/Assign** and *left-click* on the smaller shape.
7. In **3D Lofter, Shape/Get/Shaper** and the smaller polygon appears in the **Shape** viewport and also at Level 4 of the Path line in the **Top (X/Z)** viewport.
8. Press **Page Up** three more times. The 7th Level highlights and the Shape disappears from the **Shape** viewport.
9. **Shape/Get Shaper** and the Shape reappears both in the **Shape** viewport and at Level 7 of the **Top (X/Z)** viewport.

10. **Object/Make** and with **Tween** and **Contour** on, but with **Optimization** off *left-click* on **OK**.
11. **Object/Preview** to check that the 3D model is as desired.
12. In the **3D Editor** the model will appear in all viewports. It can now, if required, have lights, cameras, materials and background added and be rendered.

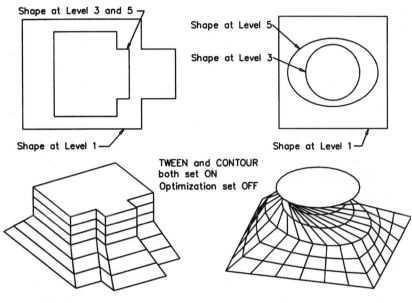

Fig. 5.20 Examples of 3D models from Shapes at different levels

Notes

1. Take care in the positioning of the vertices of the Shapes as they are created. Each polygon must have the same number of vertices and, in each polygon, the vertices should be in comparable positions. For example in the right hand example of Fig. 5.20, the vertices of the ellipse and circle are not in line with those of the parallelogram, the 3D model appears as if twisted around throughout its length;
2. **Optimization** must be off in the **Object Lofting Controls** dialogue box.

Status Line

The Status Line has been referred to earlier (page 2) when keying X and Y coordinate numbers. Depending upon which of the 3D Studio programs are in use, the content of the Status Line varies. Some examples are given in Figs 5.19 and 5.21–25.

In the 2D Shaper (Fig. 5.21): the Status Line shows: the number of polygons in the Shape (**P:**); the number of vertices in all polygons

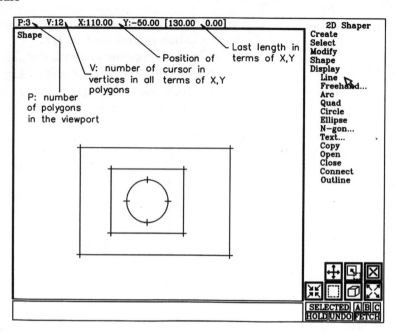

Fig. 5.21 The Status Line in the **2D Shaper** program

(**V:**); the position of the cursor in terms of X and Y (**X: Y:**) and the length of the last Segment to be created. (**[130.00: 0,0]**). In the last item the figure 130.00 is the number of X units moved and the figure 0.00, the number of Y units. In this example, the last line drawn was therefore 130 units long in the horizontal (X) direction. The 0.00 shows that the Segment was horizontal.

In the 3D Lofter (Figs 5.22–25): the content of the Status Line depends upon which of the **Deform** command is in use. The **Shape** viewport changes name to either **Scale**, **Twist**, **Teeter** or **Bevel**, depending upon which of the **Deform** commands is current, and the Status Line shows the extent of the deformation in %, degrees or movement, depending upon, for example, **Deform/Scale.../Move** or **Deform/Scale.../Insert**.

It is important when working in any of the programs of 3D Studio to watch both the Status Line and the Prompt Line. The reader is advised to experiment with the **Deform** command sets, not only to see the relevance of the figures occurring in the Status Line, but to understand the possibilities of modifying models available with these commands.

Path Shapes

A *left-click* on **Path/Get...** allows access to the shapes in the **2D Shaper** in order to get shapes for paths. In the **2D Shaper** the required Shape

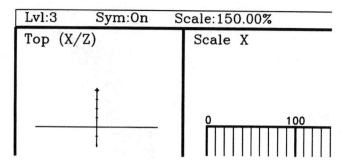

Fig. 5.22 The Status Line for
Deform/Scale...

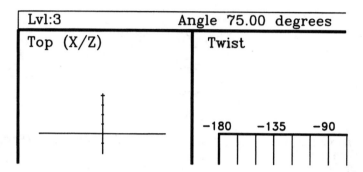

Fig 5. 23 The Status Line for
Deform/Twist...

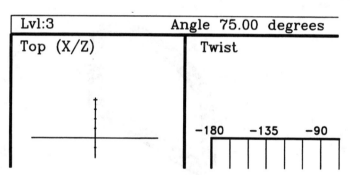

Fig. 5.24 The Status Line for
Deform/Teeter...

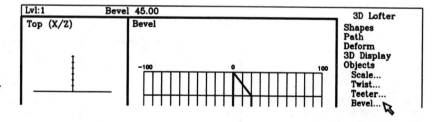

Fig. 5.25 The Status Line for
Deform/Bevel...

must first be selected with **Shape/Assign**. Then **Path/Get.../Shaper**
brings the assigned shape into the Viewports of the **3D Lofter** in which
the Path line is displayed. Several examples are given in Figures 5.26
and 5.27. The shape along the Path line is shown in these two figures
as separate drawings together with the Path line and the resulting 3D
model. The sequence in obtaining these models would be:

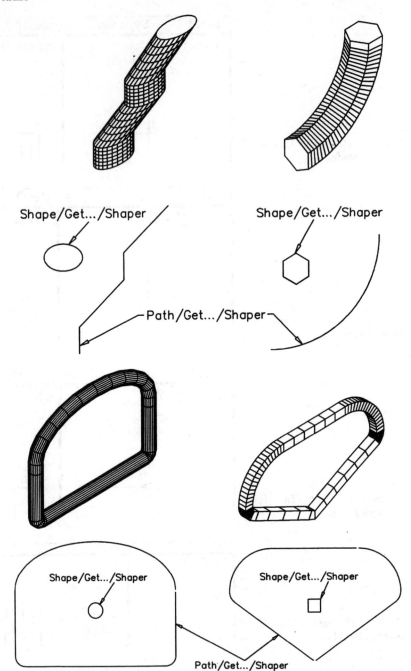

Fig. 5.26 Two examples of
path curves and the
resulting models

Fig. 5.27 Further examples of
path curves from the **2D
Shaper** in the **3D Lofter**

1. In **2D Shaper** create both the path and the shape to be lofted along
   the path.
2. **Shape/Assign** – *left-click* on the path shape.
3. In **3D Lofter** – **Path/Get.../Shaper** and the path shape appears in
   each of the viewports in which the path is present.

4. In **2D Shaper – Assign/None** followed by a *left-click* on the shape to be lofted.
5. In **3D Lofter – Shape/Get.../Shaper**, followed by repeated pressing of the **Page Up** key of the keyboard to place the shape at each vertex.

Notes

1. When creating shapes in the **2D Shaper** for lofting, time and trouble is saved if the start of a Path shape starts at the cursor position **X:0.00 Y:0.00**.
2. The lofted shape is usually easier to handle in the **3D Lofter** if its central point is at **X:0.00 Y:0.00**.
3. You may well find yourself running out of vertices at which to place the lofted shape in the **Lofter**. A warning box will appear if this happens. It is usually quite easy to avoid this if it is remembered that lines often require a shape at each end and arcs may only require a shape to be placed at the three vertices of each arc. This problem can also be overcome by setting the path steps to a smaller number than the default 5. **Path/Steps** brings up the dialogue box for this purpose.
4. If your 3D model consists of more than a single object, make sure you give a different name for each object. If this rule is not followed, each time an object is made in the **3D Lofter**, any object with the same name is deleted from the **3D Editor**. It is advisable to name each object in a model with easily identifiable names in the dialogue box appearing when **Make/Object** is selected.
5. When using **Object/Make** the shape of your model will be different with **Contour** set on to what it would be with **Contour** set off. Remember **Contour** can be set on or off by *left-clicks* on the button in the icon panel, or in the **Object Lofting Controls** dialogue box (page 78). An example of the differences is given in Fig. 5.28. Only when **Contour** is on will the shapes be at right angles to the vertices in the path. When it is off, the shapes will lie at right angles to the start point of the path.

More about the Deform command set

Fig. 5.29 shows a number of different outlines obtained from the simple model of Fig. 5.28, after being acted upon by the **Deform** commands. When applying any of the **Deform** set, it must be borne in mind that their actions are progressive, in that once any one of the deformation grids is set, its action will be coupled to that of any other deformation grid setting, unless set back to **Default**, the grid will still be active. This is shown in the last two models in Fig. 5.29, in which

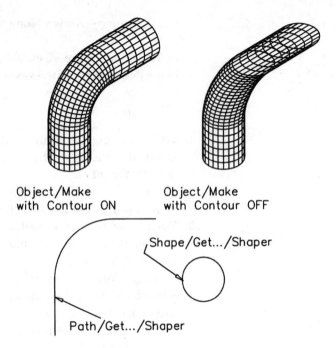

Fig. 5.28 Two models
showing the difference
between the models made
with **Contour** on or off

Deform/Scale has been set, followed by **Deform/Bevel**, then with the
first two deformation grids still in action **Deform/Teeter** has been set.

Questions

1. What is the sequence of procedures for creating a model from
   Shapes which have been created in the **2D Shaper** and then
   rendering the model?

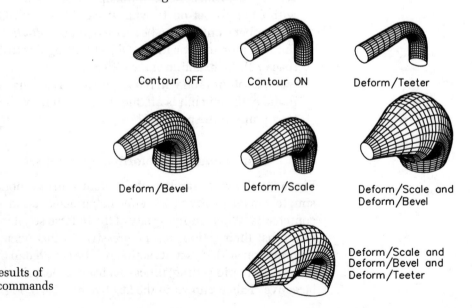

Fig. 5.29 The results of
using **Deform** commands

2. How is a solid of revolution created?
3. Why do you think it is necessary to use Spherical mapping when adding a surface to a sphere?
4. Which commands are used to create a model in a helical form?
5. What is the difference between a model lofted along a circular path with **Contour** on and the same model lofted along a circular path with **Contour** off?
6. What is a deformation grid?
7. When would **Optimization** be turned Off when lofting shapes?
8. How are extra vertices included in a path in the **3D Lofter**?
9. What happens to a lofted model when **Path Detail** and **Shape Detail** are set to LOW in the **Object Lofting Control** dialogue box?
10. How does one move a Level along a path?

Exercises

1. Fig. 5.30. In **2D Shaper** using **Create/Line** with **Snap** set to 5 and **Grid** set to 10, draw the shape to the dimensions given. In **3D Lofter**, **Shape/Get...Shaper** will bring the shape into the **Shape** viewport. In the **Surface of Revolution** dialogue box which will appear with **Path/SurfRev** set the parameters to suitable sizes and form the Surface of revolution shown in Fig. 5.30. Render the model using a surface which resembles steel.

2. Fig. 5.31. With **Path/SurfRev** and suitable settings in the **Surface of Revolution** dialogue box, create the barrel shown in Fig,. 5.31. When you have created the model, in the **3D Editor** add a top and a bottom to the barrel. Place the top in position as if it had been taken off and left on the floor beside the barrel. Now render the model with lights, camera, background and with suitable wood surfaces and mapping.

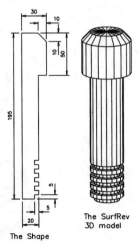

The Shape

The SurfRev
3D model

Fig. 5.30 Exercise 1

Fig. 5.31 Exercise 2

3. Fig. 5.32. A drawing (DXF file from 3D Studio **3D Editor**) and a rendering of it is given in Fig. 5.33. The model is made up from **Create/Cylinder.../Smoothing**, a **Create/LSphere.../Smoothing** and a **Create/Circle...** shape which was been lofted along a path in the shape of a quadrant arc. The model was rendered after lights, a camera, Spherical mapping and a Brass Gifmap surface had been applied. The rendering was completed against a white background (RGB: 255,255,255).

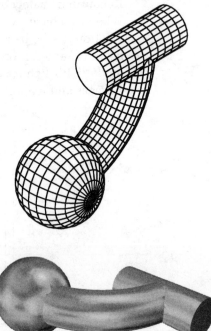

Fig. 5.32 Exercise 3

Fig. 5.33 A rendering of Exercise 3

4. Fig. 5.34. The model (again from a DXF file saved in the **3D Editor**) was created from **Create/Box, Create/Cone.../Smoothing** and a the path included as in Fig. 5.26. The model then had lights and a camera added. Surface finishes, which required Mapping, were WOOD – WHITE ASH (the base), BRASS GIFMAP (the cone) and CHROME GIFMAP (the bar). The rendering was against a white background. The rendering is shown in Fig. 5.35.

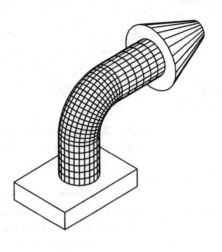

Fig. 5.34 Exercise 4

Fig. 5.35 A rendering of the model from Exercise 4

5. Fig. 5.36. This model was lofted from **Create/Quad...**, each quadri-lateral having 4 sides. In the **3D Editor** the objects **Made** from the lofted shapes were **Create/Objects.../Boolean** unioned and an **LSphere** placed on top of the stand. The resulting model had lights and a camera added, the stand was mapped with a MARBLE GREEN surface and the sphere mapped with a CHROME GIFMAP surface. The model was then rendered against a white background. The resulting rendering is shown in Fig. 5.37.

6. Fig. 5.38. The four models of Fig. 5.38 have been lofted from a variety of shapes created in **2D Shaper** and lofted in the **3D Lofter**.

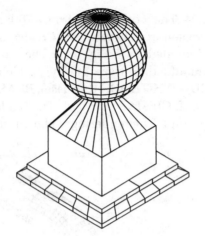

Fig. 5.36 Exercise 5

Fig. 5.37 A rendering of the model from Exercise 5

7. Fig. 5.39 shows two renderings of helices, one of which is Boolean subtracted from, and the other Boolean Unioned to, a cylinder. The details for creating these renderings were:

(a) **2D Shaper: Create/Circle.../Smoothing** of radius 10.
(b) **3D Lofter: Shape/Get.../Shaper.**
(c) **3D Lofter: Path/Helix** – Diameter Start and End 100; Height 200; Number of turns 2.5; Degrees 180; Vertices 20; CW on.
(d) **3D Lofter: Object/Make** – **Tween** and **Contour** both on.
(e) **3D Editor: Create/Cylinder.../Smoothing** – Radius 10, Height 220.
(f) **3D Editor: Create/Object.../Boolean** – First example subtract helix from cylinder; second example union helix and cylinder.

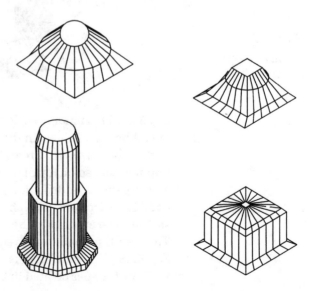

Fig. 5.38 Exercise 6

Fig. 5.39 Exercise 7

(g) **3D Editor: Surface\Materials.../Choose** – CHROME GIFMAP and apply to the object.

(h) **3D Editor: Surface/Mapping.../Type.../Cylindrical** – apply to the object.

(i) **3D Editor: Renderer/Background** – white (255,255,255).

(j) **3D Editor: Renderer/Render** – Phong, Anti-aliasing.

Expect to have to wait for several minutes for the rendering to complete once **Renderer/Render** has been selected, followed by a *left-click* in the **Camera01** viewport.

8. Fig. 5.40 shows examples of helices created by different settings of **Tween**, **Contour** and **Degrees**. Practise creating such helices with different settings similar to those shown.

Tween off   Tween off   Tween on   Tween on
Contour off   Contour on   Contour on   Contour on
                                  Degrees 0   Degrees 180

Shape: Circle of Radius 10
Path: Helix — Start and End diameters: 100
Height: 200
Number of Turns: 3

Fig. 5.40 Exercise 8

9. Fig. 5.41 shows examples of a circle from **2D Shaper** lofted in **3D Lofter** and acted upon by successive Deform commands. Practise settings of the **Path/Deform** command set similar to those shown.

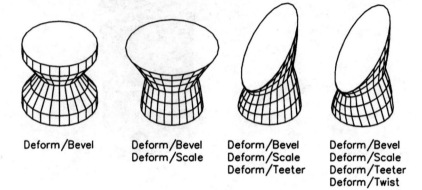

Deform/Bevel   Deform/Bevel   Deform/Bevel   Deform/Bevel
                Deform/Scale   Deform/Scale   Deform/Scale
                                Deform/Teeter   Deform/Teeter
                                                Deform/Twist

Fig. 5.41 Exercise 9

CHAPTER 6

Further examples of lofted models

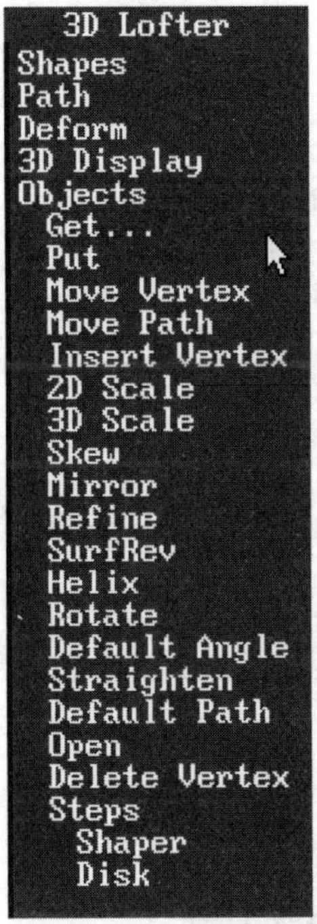

Introduction

As explained in an earlier chapter, the stages of creating a rendered 3D model completely in 3D Studio can follow the procedure:

1. Create a shape in the **2D Shaper**.
2. Loft the shape in the **3D Lofter**.
3. In the **3D Lofter** if necessary edit the path in a variety of ways and **Object/Make** the model.
4. In the **3D Editor** render the 3D model after adding lights, cameras, materials, mapping and background.

Note: 3D models created in 3D Studio consist of a series of triangular surface meshes, the vertices of which are interconnected to form complete surface meshes.

This chapter consists of a number of examples of 3D models created and rendered in 3D Studio, employing methods not fully covered in earlier chapters.

Adjusting Paths

Left-click on **Path** in the **3D Lofter** command column. The sub-set of commands appears – Fig. 6.1. Taking each of these in turn:

Get... brings up another sub-set:

> **Shaper** allows an assigned shape from **2D Shaper** to be used as a path.
>
> **Disk** allows a path file (with a file extension *.lft) to be used as a path.
>
> **Put** puts the current path as a shape into the **2D Shaper**. The dialogue box **There is a shape assigned in the 2D Shaper. What do you want to do with it?** – Fig. 6.2 – may appear.
>
> **Move Vertex** allows a vertex in the path shape to be moved. Examples are given in Figs 6.7–11.
>
> **Move Path** allows the whole path to be moved.

Fig. 6.1 The **Path** command sub-sets

Fig. 6.2 The dialogue box
which may appear when
Path/Put is selected

Insert Vertex allows a vertex to be placed in any position along the
path shape. Examples will be given later in this chapter.

2D Scale allows the path to be scaled. A *left-click* in the **Top (X/Z)**
viewport makes it current. Move the mouse with the button held
down and the scale of the path changes. Release the button when
satisfied.

3D Scale allows the path to be scaled in X, Y and Z directions.

Skew allows the path to be skewed.

Mirror allows a mirror image of the current path to be formed.

Refine allows vertices to be placed anywhere along the path.

SurfRev – examples have been given in Chapter 5.

Helix – examples have been given in Chapter 5.

Rotate allows the path shape to be rotated in degrees up to 180 in both
directions. The angle of rotation appears in the Status line as the
path shape is rotated by moving the mouse.

Default Angle restores a rotated path shape to its original angular
position.

Straighten straightens a path which has been acted upon by **Move
Vertex**. Figure 6.3 shows the dialogue box associated with this
command.

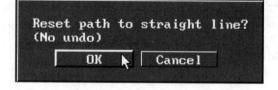

Fig. 6.3 The dialogue box
Reset path to straight line?

Default Path restores the path to the default single line 7-step path.

Open will open any selected segment of a closed path – such as a path
in the shape of a circle, an ellipse or a closed polygon.

Delete Vertex deletes a selected vertex. Will change the shape of a
closed or curved path.

Steps allows the number of steps in a path to be set – up to 10 – Fig.
6.4.

Fig. 6.4 The **Set Path Steps**
dialogue box

The following are some of the message boxes associated with the
Path command sub-set:

Put – Shaper. What do you want to do with it? dialogue box.
SurfRev – Surface of Revolution dialogue box.
Helix – Helix Path Definition dialogue box.
Default Path – Replace the current path? dialogue box.
Straighten – if a closed polygon path – **Can't straighten a closed
path** warning box.
Steps – Set Path Steps dialogue box appears when this command is
chosen.

Notes

1. If an error has been made in changing a path shape with the aid of
   any of the **Path** tools (as commands are often called), a *left-click* on
   UNDO in the Icon Panel undoes the error. But remember that a
   second *left-click* on **UNDO** will bring back the error which was
   previously undone.
2. As with other operations in 3D Studio, the reader is advised to
   watch both the Status line and the Prompt line when using any of
   these tools. Angles and distances will appear in the Status line and
   prompts stating what has to be done to carry out an operation
   appear in the Prompt line.
3. Until one becomes accustomed to making entries in the dialogue
   boxes associated with these tools, take some care in deciding what
   the entries should be.
4. It is easy to confuse the two sets of tools **Shapes** and **Path** in the **3D
   Lofter** command column. The tools named above are from the **Path**
   sets.

Examples of models using Path settings

First example – moving a vertex in the path

This example is of a shape created in the **2D Shaper** and lofted in the
3D Lofter along a path in which a vertex has been moved. The
sequence to produce the final rendered model was:

Fig. 6.5 The Switch viewports icon from the **3D Lofter** Icon Panel

1. In **2D Shaper** create the required shape.
2. In **3D Lofter** with **Shapes/Get.../Shaper** bring the shape into the Lofter.
3. *Left-click* on the viewports switch icon in the icon panel (Fig. 6.5) to exchange the **Top (X/Z)** viewport with the **Shape** viewport.
4. In the **Top (X/Z)** viewport, press the **S** key to set Snap.
5. **Path/Insert Vertex** and insert a vertex at Level 4 of the path.
6. **Path/Move Vertex**. With the unidirectional cursor set horizontally (Tab key), move the new vertex 30 units in the negative X direction.
7. **Objects/Make**. With **Tween** off, *left-click* on **Create** in the **Objects Lofting Controls** dialogue box.
8. Check that the model mesh is as desired with **Object/Preview**. Change the path vertices if necessary with **Path/Move Vertex**.
9. When satisfied that a good 3D model mesh has been made, press **F3** to get into the **3D Editor**.
10. Add lights, a camera, a material and a background and render the model.

Fig. 6.7 shows the 3D model mesh and Fig. 6.8 the rendered model in the material CHROME GIFMAP.

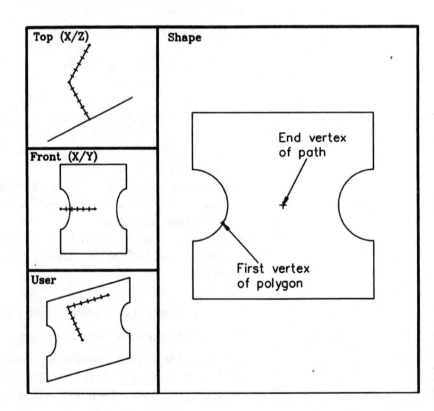

Fig. 6.6 The **3D Lofter** screen for the first example

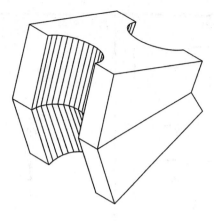

Fig. 6.7 The 3D model mesh
of the first example

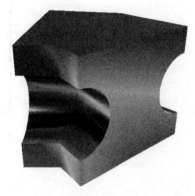

Fig. 6.8 The rendered model
of the first example

Second example – moving a path vertex to form a curve

In this example a vertex has been placed in the path and then moved
in such a manner to form the path into a curve. The sequence leading
up to the final rendered 3D model was as follows:

1. Create a Shape in the **2D Shaper** and in **3D Lofter** with **Shapes/
   Get.../Shaper** bring the shape into the **3D Lofter**. *Left-click* on the
   viewports switch icon in the icon panel:
2. **Path/Insert Vertex**. Insert a vertex at Level 4 of the Path.
3. **Path/Move Vertex**. Set the unidirectional cursor to allow movement in any direction. *Left-click* on the new vertex and drag it 20
   units in a negative X direction. Do not yet *right-click,* which would
   release the vertex from mouse movement.
4. While holding the mouse button down, move the mouse vertically.
   Two coloured lines ending in arrows appear. These are tangential
   to a curve of the path which changes shape as the mouse is moved.
   When satisfied that the curve is of a required shape, release the
   mouse button. Fig. 6.9 shows the path curve as it is being formed
   – i.e. while the mouse button is being held down.
5. **Objects/Make**. In the **Objects Lofting Controls** dialogue box, set
   Tween on and *left-click* on **Create**.
6. Press **F3** and check in the **3D Editor** that the 3D model mesh is as
   desired or, in **3D Lofter**, **Objects/Preview** will give a 3D visualisa-
   tion of the mesh which has been acted upon with **Objects/Make**.

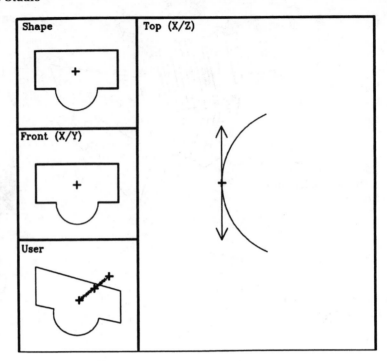

Fig. 6.9 The **3D Lofter** screen
for example 2

7. If satisfied with the mesh go on to rendering. If not amend the Path curve.
8. Add lights, a camera, a material and a background and render the mesh.

Fig. 6.10 shows the 3D model mesh and Fig. 6.11 a rendering.

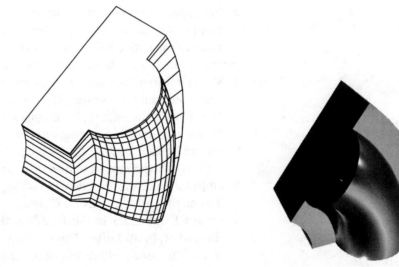

Fig. 6.10 The 3D model
mesh resulting from a
curved Path of the second
example

Fig. 6.11 The rendered
model of the second
example

Plate I A rendering of the three glasses scene (Chapter 2) in Wire shading

Plate II A rendering of the three glasses scene (Chapter 2) in Flat shading

Plate III   A rendering
of the three glasses
scene (Chapter 2) in
Phong shading

Plate IV   A rendering
of Exercise 1 (Chapter 7)

Plate V A rendering of the second example in Chapter 8

Plate VI A rendering of the fourth example in Chapter 7

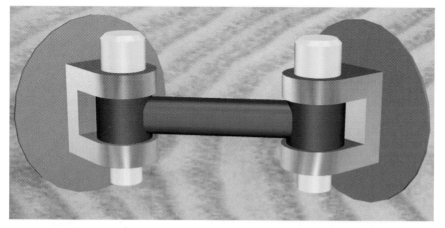

Plate VII   A rendering of an engineering component created wholly within 3D Studio

Plate VIII   A rendering of Exercise 5, Chapter 5

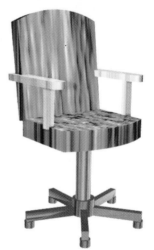

Plate IX   A rendering of a chair – first example in Chapter 9

Plate X   A rendering of three meshing gears constructed in AutoCAD and loaded into 3D Studio via the DXF facility – eighth example in Chapter 8

Plate XI A rendering of a sphere onto which the Jupiter.tga file has been spherically mapped. The background is a cloud scene from the CD-ROM of 3D Studio Release 2

Plate XII A rendering of the Japanese umbrella from Chapter 9

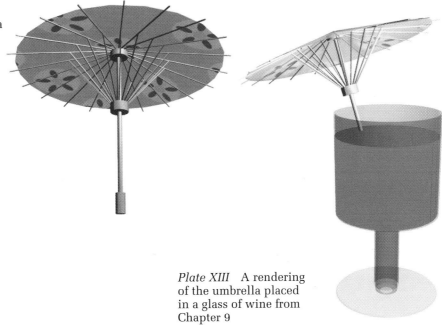

Plate XIII A rendering of the umbrella placed in a glass of wine from Chapter 9

Plate XIV A rendering of the kitchen scene – seventh example in Chapter 8

Plate XV Another rendering of the kitchen scene after moving the camera

Plate XVI A rendering of the room project in Chapter 10

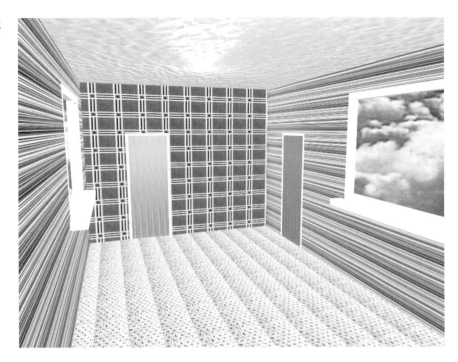

Plate XVII A rendering of the table within a room scene – fifth example in Chapter 8

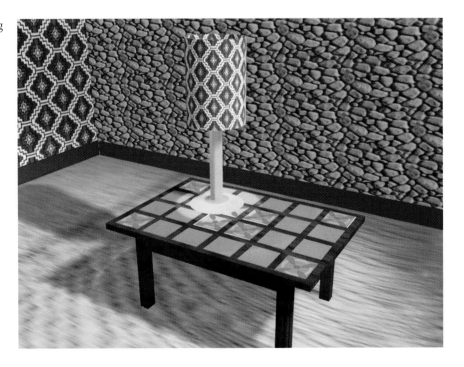

Plate XVIII A rendering of the wall switch – second example in Chapter 3

Plate XIX A rendering of Christmas decorations – sixth example in Chapter 8

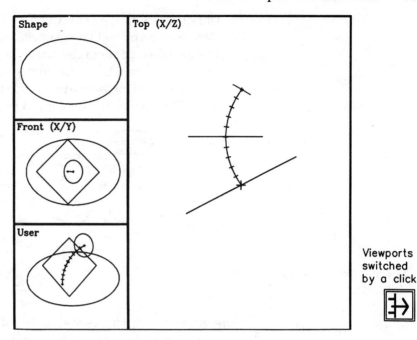

Fig. 6.12 The 3D Lofter
screen for the third example

Viewports
switched
by a click

Third example – a model from shapes at several levels along a curved path

1. In **2D Shaper** create three Shapes – a **Create/Ellipse**, a **Create/Quad** and a **Create/Circle**. **Object.../Polygon.../Rotate** the shapes until the start vertices of each shape (small blue cross on the shape outline) are in a common position relative to each shape.
2. **Shape/Assign** the ellipse.
3. **F2** to get into the **3D Lofter**. **Shapes/Get.../Shaper** brings the ellipse at the bottom vertex of the Path. *Left-click* on the switch viewports icon.
4. **Path/Insert Vertex** and **Path/Move Vertex** and form the path into a curve as in the second Example.
5. **F1** into the **2D Shaper**. **Shape/Assign**. *Left-click* on the ellipse, which de-assigns it. *Left-click* on the quadrilateral to assign it.
6. **F2** into the **3D Lofter**. Press the **Page Up** key of the keyboard until the central vertex of the Path is highlighted and **Lvl:7 appears** in the Status Line.
7. **Shapes/Get.../Shaper** and the quadrilateral appears at the highlighted vertices of the path.
8. **F1** back to the **2D Shaper**. De-assign the quad and assign the circle.
9. **F2** back to the **3D Lofter**. **Page Up** to the top vertex of the path.
10. **Shapes/Get.../Shaper** and the circle appears at the top vertex of the path.

11. **Object/Make**. In the **Object Lofting Controls** dialogue box, turn **Optimization** off and **Tween** on, followed by a *left-click* on **Create**.

12. **F3** into the **3D Editor** to check that the 3D model mesh is OK. If not go back to amend the lofting process.

13. When satisfied render the model mesh. Fig. 6.13 shows the model mesh. The rendered model is not illustrated here.

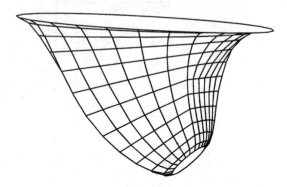

Fig. 6.13 The 3D mesh of the third example

Note: When placing shapes at a number of positions along a path, each shape must have the same number of vertices. If shapes without an equal number of vertices are attempted to be placed along the path the warning box illustrated in Fig. 6.14 appears and the shapes cannot be placed as desired.

Fig. 6.14 The warning box stating that all shapes must have the same number of vertices

All shapes must have the same
number of vertices.

Continue

Fourth example – a model created along a Path/Fit... path

1. In **2D Shaper** create two shapes, one of which is a circle of any diameter, the second is a polygon which will be the path for the 3D mesh.

2. **Assign** the circle.

3. **F2** into the **3D Lofter**. **Shapes/Get.../Shaper** and the circle shape appears.

4. **F1** back to the **2D Shaper**. **Assign** polygon and de-assign the circle.

5. **F2** into the **3D Lofter**. **Path/Deform/Get.../Shaper**. The **3D Lofter** screen now appears as in Fig. 6.15. Note there are now two viewports named **Fit X** and **Fit Y** in which the polygon shape now appears. Note also the lines of the path levels across the shape in the **Fit X** viewports.

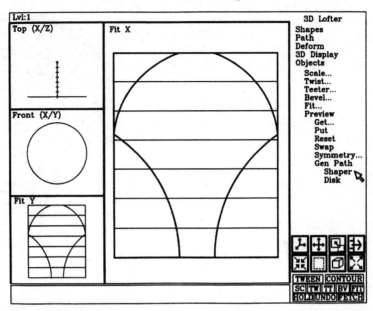

Fig. 6.15 The **3DLofter**
screen for the fourth
example after **Path/Deform/
Get.../Shaper**

6. **Path/Deform/Fit.../Gen Path** and the **Fit X** and **Fit Y** viewports
change as shown in Fig. 6.15.

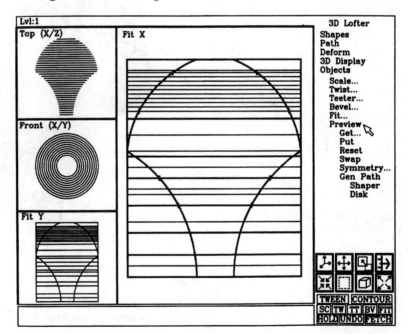

Fig. 6.16 The **3D Lofter**
screen for the fourth
example after **Path/Deform/
Fit.../Gen path**

7. **Object/Make**, followed by **Object/Preview** and the screen appears
as in Fig. 6.16.

8. **F3** into the **3D Editor** to check the mesh. If satisfied the mesh can
now be rendered. Fig. 6.17 shows the 3D model mesh and Fig. 6.18
the rendered 3D model.

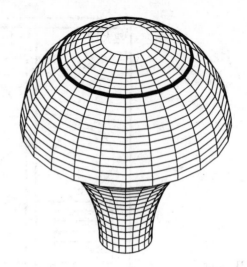

Fig. 6.17 the 3D Model mesh
for the fourth example

Fig. 6.18 The rendering of
the fourth example

Fifth example – another Path/Fit example

Another example of a 3D mesh is shown in Fig. 6.19. The polygon
forming the Path is shown in Fig. 6.20. The shape taken into the **3D
Lofter** for the plan of the 3D mesh was an **N-Gon.../Flat** of 6 sides. The
method for creating this example followed the same sequence as for
Example 4.

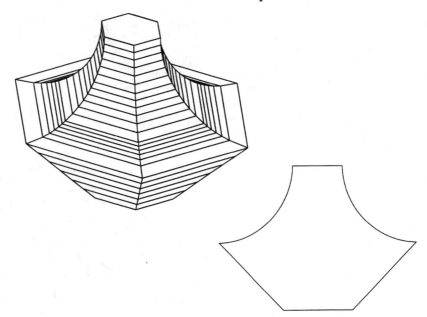

Fig. 6.19 The 3D model
mesh of the fifth example

Fig. 6.20 The polygon for the
Path of the fifth example

Fig. 6.21 Sixth example – the
rendered guitar

Sixth example – a guitar body from a number of shapes

The shapes from each part of this example were lofted separately in the
3D Lofter after being independently **Assigned** in the **2D Shaper**. They
were then moved and rotated in position in the **3D Editor** before being
rendered. The Shapes and the height of their loftings are given in Fig.
6.22 and the rendered image in Fig. 6.21. Shapes such as those shown
are easily created in the **2D Shaper** with **Create/Line** followed by
Modify/Vertex.../Move and using the move tool to not only move
vertices but also to spline curve them. Hold down the mouse button
after moving; two spline adjusting arrows appear. Drag the mouse and
adjust the spline curve at the chosen vertex. A variety of materials were
chosen for the parts of the guitar, most of which had to be mapped onto
the parts. The resulting 3D model was rendered against a white
background. It should be noted here that most of the renderings shown
in this book have been rendered against white backgrounds, except for
those in the colour plates. This is because when printed in black and
white as on this white paper, a white background allows the rendered
models to show up more clearly.

Seventh example – text on a curved surface

This example was the result of **Create/Text.../Font, Create/Text.../
Enter** and **Create/Text.../Place** in the **2D Shaper**, followed by assigning
all the letters and then lofting them in the **3D Lofter**. Then, in the **3D**

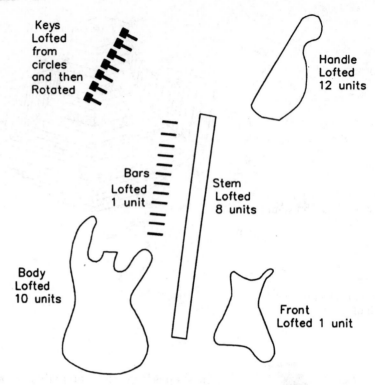

Keys
Lofted
from
circles
and then
Rotated

Handle
Lofted
12 units

Bars
Lofted
1 unit

Stem
Lofted
8 units

Body
Lofted
10 units

Front
Lofted 1 unit

Fig. 6.22 The Shapes for the guitar body - sixth example

Editor, a cylinder was created, which was **Create/Objects.../Boolean** intersected with the text, to produce a curved front surface on the text. A second cylinder was then **Create/Object.../Boolean** subtracted from the text to form the curved text – Fig. 6.23 shows the stages in creating this example and Fig. 6.24 shows the resultant rendering after lights, camera, material and a background were included with the object.

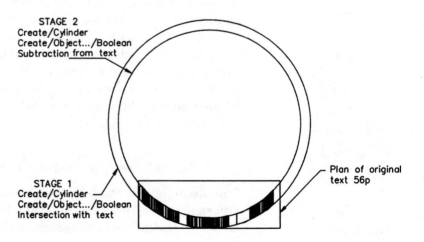

STAGE 2
Create/Cylinder
Create/Object.../Boolean
Subtraction from text

Plan of original
text 56p

STAGE 1
Create/Cylinder
Create/Object.../Boolean
Intersection with text

Fig. 6.23 Stages in creating the 3D mesh for the seventh example

Fig. 6.24 A rendering of the seventh example

Eighth example – a 'gold' ring with a message

Following a similar procedure as for the seventh Example by creating the text, **Create/Object.../Boolean** intersecting it with a cylinder, following by **Create/Tube.../Smooth** to add a ring behind the text. Different materials were then assigned to the two parts of the ring, which was rendered after adding lights, a camera and a background to the object in the **3D Editor**. Fig. 6.25 shows the stages in creating the ring and Fig. 6.26 is a rendering of the completed object.

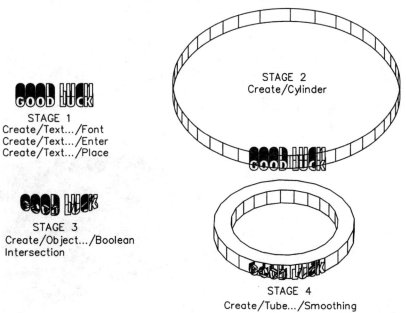

STAGE 1
Create/Text.../Font
Create/Text.../Enter
Create/Text.../Place

STAGE 2
Create/Cylinder

STAGE 3
Create/Object.../Boolean
Intersection

STAGE 4
Create/Tube.../Smoothing

Fig. 6.25 Stages in creating the 3D model mesh for the eighth example

Ninth example – an anvil

To create the 3D model mesh for this example, the main body of the anvil was constructed from a shape in **2D Shaper**, lofted in **3D Lofter**.

Fig. 6.26 A rendering of the
eighth example

The conical part was constructed following the methods explained
with Examples 4 and 5, using **Path/Deform/Get.../Shaper** and **Path/
Deform/Put.../Gen Shape** in the **3D Lofter**, using the outline of the
conical part as a path. Fig. 6.27 is a 3D model mesh of the anvil and Fig.
6.28 a rendering, after lights, a camera, material and a background had
been included in the **3D Editor**.

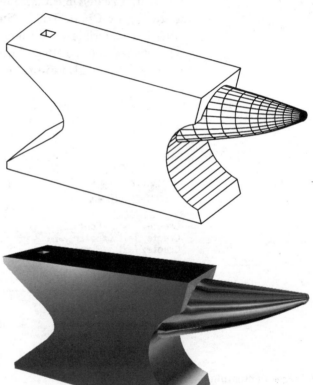

Fig. 6.27 3D Model mesh for
the ninth example

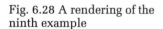

Fig. 6.28 A rendering of the
ninth example

Exercises

Attempt all the examples given in this chapter following the descriptions given with each example.

CHAPTER 7

The Materials Editor

Introduction

In any of the 3D Studio programs described in earlier chapters, press the **F5** key of the keyboard or *left-click* on **Program** in the menu bar, followed by another *left-click* on **Materials** in the pull-down menu,. and the **Materials Editor** screen appears (Fig. 7.1). It will be noted that the screen has a resolution of 600 pixels by 350 pixels. The purpose of the program is to enable the operator to create his/her own surface materials for inclusion in a rendering of a 3D solid model. Existing materials can also be edited if required – for example their colour can be changed, their mapping types can be amended. In this chapter, examples showing the creation of materials for adding labels, for creating new materials and for editing existing materials are included to give an introduction to the facilities available with the **Materials Editor**. The **Materials Editor** screen shows the following:

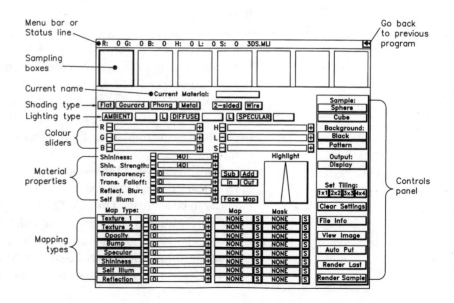

Fig. 7.1 The **Materials Editor** program screen

Menu bar or Status line: This shows either the status of the colours chosen, their intensities and the materials library currently loaded, or the names of the pull-down menus available with the editor – **Info**, **Library**, **Material**, **Options** and **Program**.

Sampling boxes: Seven sampling boxes appear just below the Status bar. As will be seen later, sample rendering on spheres or cubes will appear in these boxes to give a visual check of the materials which are being made in the editor. *Left-click* in any one of the boxes to make it the current box in which the currently created material will be displayed on a sphere (or cube). Rendered spheres (or cubes) can be transferred between sampling boxes by *dragging* with the mouse. A dialogue box assists this action, but take care – your created material may be lost if it has not been saved.

Current name: The name of the material which has been created, or the name of the material being edited shows below the sampling boxes.

Shading levels: These are the same shading levels as set when rendering and show the rendering of the currently created material to appear on a sphere (or cube) in the selected sampling box. After the settings for the material have been made, the sampling box can show **Flat**, **Gourard**, **Phong** or **Metal** shading. If necessary **2-sided** shading can also be given to the material.

Lighting: A *left-click* on **Ambient** allows the **RGB** and/or the **HLS** sliders to be set in order to set the colour and intensity of the ambient lighting for the material. Similarly *left-clicks* on either **Diffuse** or **Specular** allows the setting of the sliders for these forms of light. To the right of each of the light type names is an empty box, which changes colour as the settings are made with the aid of the sliders. **Specular** is not available for **Metal** shading.

Sliders for colour settings: These sliders for **R** (Red), **G** (Green), **B** (Blue), **H** (Hue), **L** (Luminosity) and **S** (Saturation), allow settings for each component. Once set the colours can be locked – *left-click* on the button marked **L**, followed by a *left-click* on **OK** in the **Lock Ambient and Diffuse?** or the **Lock Diffuse and Specular?** dialogue boxes. The colours relating to the **R**, **G**, **B**, **H**, **L**, **S** settings show in the buttons to the right of the lighting boxes. More about these colour components later.

Shininess: Two sliders **Shininess** and **Shin. Strength** allow the shininess of the material and the size of the shininess highlight of the material to be set from 0 to 100. The highlight becomes smaller, the larger the figure set by the slider. Associated with the shininess is a window labelled **Highlight** which shows the extent of the highlight – changing automatically as the sliders are adjusted. The shininess can be softened by a *left-click* on the button labelled **Soften**.

Transparency: Two sliders allow **Transparency** and **Transparency Falloff**. The **Falloff** is either **In**side or **Out**side the material to be set. When set to 0, there is no transparency. Set at 100, trans-parency is such that the material will probably be invisible. The two buttons **Sub** and **Add**, subtract or add transparency to the object relative to the background on which it is placed. If subtracted, the material becomes transparent against the background.

Types of mapping: The material can have mapping qualities included by selection of the appropriately named button. When one of the buttons is selected, it highlights to red. The degree of mapping is set with the sliders to the right of the mapping names. When any of the buttons labelled **NONE** are selected with a *left-click*, a **Select Texture Map** dialogue box (Fig. 7.2) appears from which a file (*.tga, *.gif, *.cel etc.) can be selected for inclusion with a material, or for editing a chosen texture map as a material. The selected filename replaces the **NONE** on the button. Note that several types of map can be added to each material being created if wished. Masks can also be added in the same way. A *left-click* on any of the buttons labelled **S** brings up the **Mapping Parameters** dialogue box (Fig. 7.3);

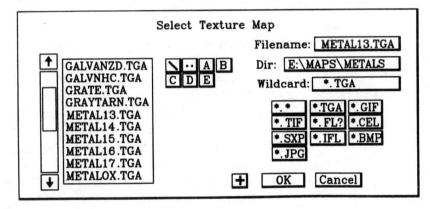

Fig 7.2 The **Select Texture** dialogue box appearing with a *left-click* on any of the **NONE** buttons

Control panel: The various features controlling the way in which the material being created is used can be set by the Control panel buttons. Sampling boxes can show the material on **Sphere** or **Cube** samples; the background can be **Black** or a **Pattern**; the **Tiling** for the mapping can be set to any one of four parameters; **File Info** can be shown on any file selected for mapping; a chosen mapping file can be viewed from **View Image** before it is applied; the **Last** or current

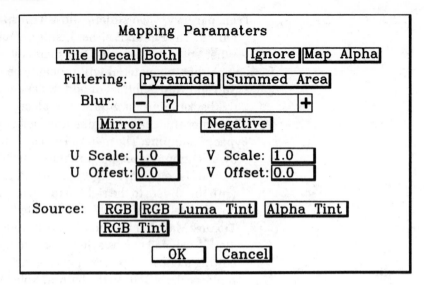

Fig. 7.3 The **Mapping Parameters** dialogue box appearing with a *left-click* on any of the **S** buttons

material can be rendered in a sampling box following a *left-click* on **Render Sample**.

Notes

Colours: R is for red; **G** is for green; **B** is for blue. Combinations of these colours will produce any required colour, which will show in the boxes next to the names **Ambient**, **Diffuse** and **Specular**.

Ambient lighting is the general all round lighting of the area containing the object(s) being lit.

Diffuse lighting is the colour of the light of the coloured part of the object to which the material is being applied.

Specular light is the highlighted light area of the object.

Hue, the actual colour, is set by the **H** slider.

Luminance, the brightness of the colour, is set by the **L** slider.

Saturation, the quality of the colour, is set by the **S** slider.

Note: all six sliders may require to be set to obtain the desired colour effect. The reader is advised to experiment with the settings of the six colour sliders until he/she is satisfied of the effects they can achieve.

Decal is applied to a material which is being created to be applied to all of an object or area. A decal material is not tiled.

Tile is applied to a material which can be applied as tiles can be applied – in a series of squares or rectangles which repeat the pattern of the material.

Examples of the use of the Materials Editor

First example

Fig. 7.4 shows the result of adding a material created in the **Materials Editor** and mapped onto a cylinder created in the **3D Editor** and then rendered. The material for this example was created in the **Materials Editor** in the following sequence:

Fig. 7.4 The rendering for the first example

1. In the **2D Shaper** with **Create/Text.../Font**, **Create/Text.../Enter** and **Create/Font.../Place** create a suitable text – Fig. 7.5. The font for this example was SWISSBLD.FNT.
2. **Shape/Assign/All** and assign all the text.
3. Press **F3** and in the **3D Editor**, **Create/Object.../Get Shape** and get the shape, set **Ambient Light** to 120, a camera, the material COLOR01 and a white background. Then **render**. **Save** to a filename such as TEXT.TGA – Fig. 7.6.

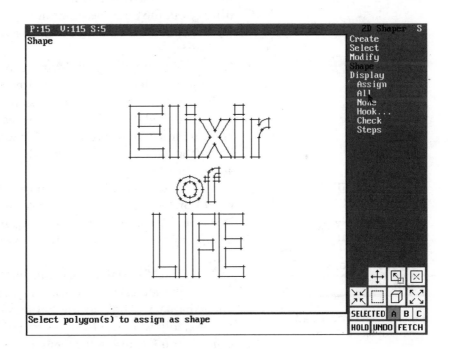

Fig. 7.5 Creating suitable text

4. Press the **F5** key to switch to the **Materials Editor**. In the editor, *left-click* on **Texture1**, *left-click* on **NONE** and load the file **TEXT.TGA** which has just been saved. Then experiment with settings of the various colour sliders, rendering different sets of settings in each of the specimen boxes in turn. Render with different types of shadings. Some practice ideas are:

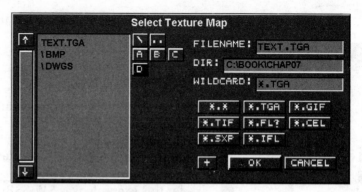

Fig. 7.6 Save the text to a
suitable filename

(a) With **Face** maps.

(b) *Left-click* on the **S** button next to the map filename and
experiment with **Decal**, **Tile** and **Both** buttons selected in the
dialogue box.

(c) Experiment with **Tile** settings of 2×2, 3×3 and 4×4.

(d) Try out the **Shininess:** settings.

(e) Try rendering to a cube as well as a sphere in the sampling
boxes.

5. Check, by calling the pull-down menu **Configure** from the **Info**
name in the Menu bar, that the directory you are going to save
materials in exists in the **Map Paths**. If necessary add a map path.

6. When satisfied that suitable renderings have been achieved, *left-
click* in the sampling box containing what is considered to be the
best of the renderings. The colour slider settings for that rendering
automatically reappear.

7. *Left-click* on **Library** in the menu bar, followed by a *left-click* on
Load library in the pull-down menu which appears – Fig. 7.7.

8. In the **Select a Material Filename to Save** dialogue box, *left-click*
on one of your own libraries or enter a suitable library name – Fig.
7.8.

9. *Left-click* on **Material** in the menu bar, followed by a second *left-
click* on **Put material** in the pull-down menu – Fig. 7.9.

10. *Enter* the name TEXT in the **Put material** dialogue box which
appears, followed by a *left-click* on **OK** – Fig. 7.10.

11. *Left-click* on **Library** in the menu bar. *Left-click* on **Save Library**
and save the library to a filename of you own.

12. The material is now loaded into a library, which can be called in
the **3D Editor** with **Surface/Material.../Get Library** from which
the material can be assigned to an object with **Surface/Material.../
Assign...** and **Surface/Material.../Mapping.../Apply**. The object
already created in the **3D Editor** for this example was a cylinder
– Fig. 7.11.

Fig. 7.7 The **Library** pull-
down menu

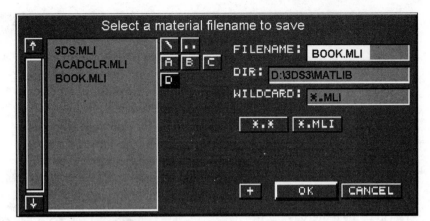

Fig. 7.8 The **Select a materials filename to save** dialogue box

Material Options	
Get material	G
Put material	P
Remove material	R
Get from scene	F
Put to scene	T
Put to current	C

Fig. 7.9 The **Material** pull-down menu

Fig. 7.10 The **Put Material** dialogue box

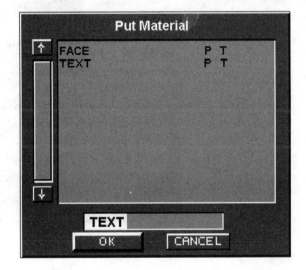

13. Because the material which was created in the **Materials Editor** is a texture map, it will have to be mapped onto the cylinder using **Surface/Mapping.../Type.../Planar** – the mapping being applied to only that part of the cylinder onto which the text is to be applied.
14. Add lights and a camera and render the model.
15. Fig. 7.12 and Fig. 7.13 show further renderings on cubes with two of the materials created in the **Materials Editor** using the file TEXT.TGA.

Second example

The rendering of this second example, which is left to the reader to attempt, is shown in Fig. 7.14. The 3D mesh for the vase, together with

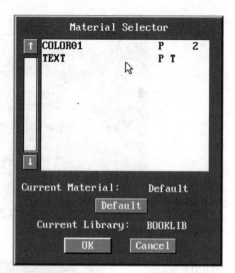

Fig. 7.11 The material created in the **Materials Editor** chosen from the **Material Selector** dialogue box

Fig. 7.12 The created material mapped onto a cube without the **Face** button having been selected

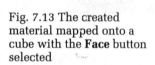

Fig. 7.13 The created material mapped onto a cube with the **Face** button selected

the shapes for the material mapped onto the vase as a label, are shown in Fig. 7.15. The vase had the material BLUE MARBLE cylindrically mapped onto its lid. The materials for the texture map for the label were colours taken from the ACADCLR.LIB library. The label was created as a Texture1 map in the **Materials Editor** and saved in the same library as that for the first example. The label was then planar mapped onto part of the surface of the vase body. A texture, from the file SAMPLES/MAPS/PATTERNS/WEAVE001.TGA to be found on the CD-ROM disk supplied with 3D Studio Release 2, was included as a background to the rendered vase.

Fig. 7.14 A rendering of the
second example

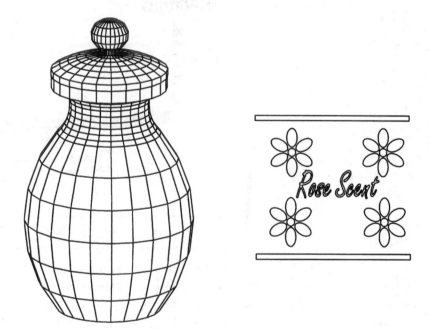

Fig. 7.15 The 3D mesh for
the vase and the design for
the material created in the
Materials Editor for the
second example

Third example

Fig. 7.16 shows the 3D mesh for this example and Fig. 7.17 shows the
final rendering. The model is a three-dimensional flow chart of the
route by which a rendering is produced in 3D Studio. Four materials
were created in the **Materials Editor** for this example:

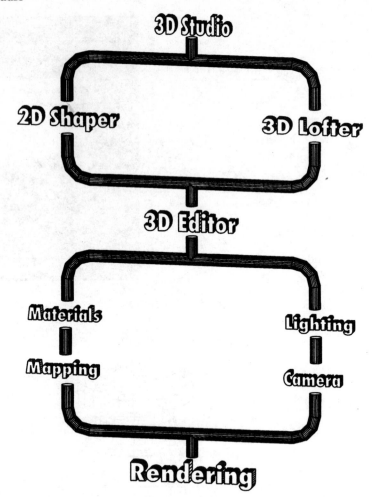

Fig. 7.16 The 3D model mesh for the third example

	Ambient	Diffuse	Secular	Shininess	Shade	Texture1
BLUE MT:	Blue	Blue	Grey	42	Phong	R 53%
MAUVE MT:	Mauve	Mauve	White	15	Phong	None
RED BALL:	Red	Red	White	22	Phong	None
RED GALV:	Red	Red	White	17	Phong	Galvanzd.tga

The file GALVANZD.TGA was taken from the CD-ROM supplied with 3D Studio Release 3.

The materials applied to the various parts of the flow chart were:

3D Studio: BLUE MT.
2D Shaper, 3D Lofter: MAUVE MT.
Materials, Mapping, Lighting, Camera: RED BALL.

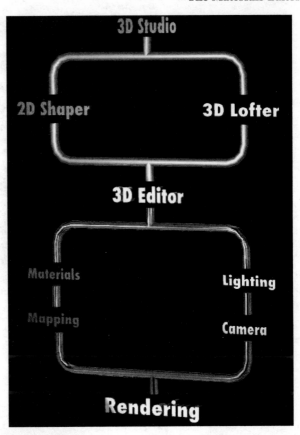

Fig. 7.17 A rendering of the third example

Rendering: RED CAM.

3D Editor and the lower piping: CHROME GIFMAP from the 3DS library.

Upper piping: GOLD (DARK) from the 3DS library.

Planar Mapping: was applied to the whole chart.

Camera: was set with a 200 mm lens with a Field of View (FOV) of 12 deg.

Background: was set for blue.

Fourth example

The fourth example, a rendering of which is given in Fig. 7.18, entailed the editing of existing materials from the materials library 3DS.MLI in the **Materials Editor** and then putting and saving the edited materials with new names in a materials library of one's own naming – I used the name BOOK.MLI, a name designed to show that materials were required in making illustrations for this book. The shapes from which the mesh was obtained are given in Fig. 7.19. The names given to the new materials edited from existing materials are shown in Fig. 7.20.

Fig. 7.18 A rendering of the
fourth example

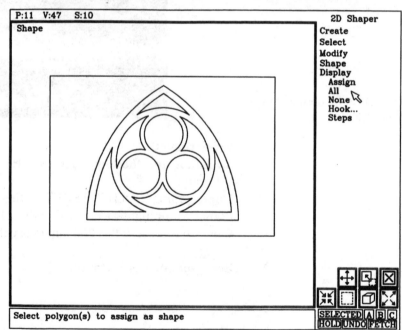

Fig. 7.19 The shapes for the
fourth example created from
Create/Circle, **Create/Arc**
and **Create/Line**

These were edited from materials in the 3DS.MLI library as follows:

1. The material **BLUE GLASS** was edited to give the three new
   materials **PURPLE GLASS**, **LGREEN GLASS** and **LBLUE GLASS**.
   BLUE GLASS was loaded into the **Materials Editor** and some of its
   parameters were changed:

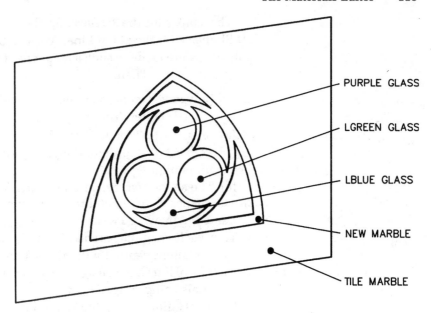

PURPLE GLASS

LGREEN GLASS

LBLUE GLASS

NEW MARBLE

TILE MARBLE

Fig. 7.20 The 3D mesh which was rendered to produce the fourth example, together with the names of the materials assigned to the parts of the mesh

Shininess: In each new material changed to 30.
Transparency: In each new material changed to 70.
Tile, 2-sided and **Phong:** Retained.
Ambient and **Diffuse:** Changed to purple, light green and light blue respectively.
Specular: In each case was retained as white.

2. The material **PINK GRAY.TGA** from the CD-ROM was edited to give the material **NEW MARBLE**. GRAY MARBLE was loaded into the **Materials Editor** and:

    Texture1: changed to 50.
    Shininess: changed to 35.
    Ambient and Diffuse: changed to green.
    Specular: White.
    Tile and **Phong:** unchanged.

3. A *left-click* on the **Current material:** button brought up the **New name for material** dialogue box. The new name GRAY MARBLE was entered as a title.

4. The material **BLUE MARBLE** was edited to give the material TILE MARBLE. The material BLUE MARBLE was loaded into the **Materials Editor** and:

    Ambient and Diffuse: Changed to a deeper grey.
    Other parameters: Left unchanged.

The shapes for the 3D mesh for this example were created in the **2D Shaper** with the aid of **Line**, **Arc** and **Circle** from **Create**. The 11 polygons were made in such a manner as to ensure that they were all closed polygons. Then:

1. All polygons except the outer rectangle were assigned and taken into the **3D Lofter**. Then:
   (a) Snap set to 2 for X, Y and Z.
   (b) Path set 0 steps, and the path vertex moved to form a path 2 units high.
   (c) The shapes were centred – **Shape/Center**.
2. The shapes were lofted through 2 units with **3D Objects/Make** to a name **MAIN** with **Tween** off.
3. Then each set of shapes was assigned and **Shape/Get.../Shaper** into the **3D Lofter**, centred with **Shape/Center** and lofted 2 units after each set of lofts had been given a new name – e.g. the colours of the materials being assigned to them.
4. In the **3D Editor** each of the 3D meshes was assigned a material (Fig. 7.20) and mapping was applied. In the case of the TILE MARBLE material of the wall, mapping was tiled to 4 × 4.
5. Finally the 3D mesh was rendered with **Phong**, **Anti-alias**, **2-sided**, **Tile** set and saved as the last image to the file name **window.tga**.

Note: It is particularly important when dealing with a series of shapes, such as those in the fourth example, to ensure that each set of shapes is centred in the **2D Lofter** before being **3D Objects/Made**. If this precaution is not taken, the shapes may become badly positioned in the **3D Editor**.

Questions

1. How many colour slider settings are there in the **Materials Editor**?
2. What is the resolution in pixels of the **Materials Editor** screen in 3D Studio Release 2?
3. What shows in the Status line of the **Materials Editor**?
4. What shows in the Menu bar of the **Materials Editor**?
5. For what purposes are the **Shininess** and **Transparency** sliders set in the **Materials Editor**?
6. State the difference between **Tile** and **Decal**.
7. What is **Specular** lighting?
8. What is the difference between **Ambient** and **Diffuse** lighting?
9. State the sequence of events to ensure that a material you have made in the **materials Editor** is saved in a library.
10. Which do you prefer – sampling to a sphere or sampling to a cube?

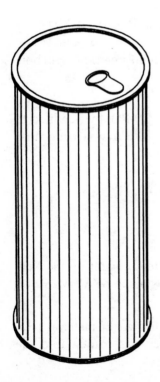

Fig. 7.21 The 3D mesh for Exercise 1

BRASS GIFMAP

MAUVE PLASTIC

RED PLASTIC

GREEN PLASTIC

BLUE PLASTC

Fig. 7.22 The label made as a material for Exercise 1 in the **Materials Editor**

Exercises

1. Fig. 7.21 is a 3D mesh for a drinks can made up from four parts: the body, top, bottom and pull-to-open catch. The top, bottom and catch are mapped with BRASS GIFMAP. A label, as a material in the **Materials Editor**, is shown in Fig. 7.22, including the names of the materials used. Fig. 7.23 is a rendering of the 3D mesh with the label mapped onto the can. The sizes, fonts and text used for the label are left to your discretion. A background was taken from the 3D Studio Release 2 CD-ROM (SAMPLES/MAPS/CLOUDS/CLOUD03.TGA).

Fig. 7.23 A rendering of Exercise 1

Fig. 7.24 Rendering of
Exercise 2

2. Fig. 7.24. Construct the 3D mesh for this exercise and create a label
   in the **Materials Editor**. The fonts, the wording of the labels for both
   the drinks can and the hoarding are left to your own discretion.
   Include a suitable background for the rendering.
3. The geometrical pattern, Fig. 7.25, was constructed in the **2D
   Shaper** taken into the **3D Editor** and materials were added as
   indicated. The pattern was then saved as a *.tga file and used in five
   materials created in the **Materials Editor**. The five materials were
   then each mapped onto a cube and rendered and tiled with a white
   background. The result of the five renderings are shown in Fig.
   7.26.

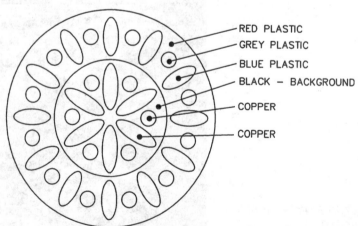

Fig. 7.25 The shapes for
Exercise 3 showing the
materials applied to the
shapes

Fig. 7.26 The five renderings for Exercise 3

Top left: Decal. Planar mapping icon same size as face of cube;
Top right: Tile and Face. Planar mapping icon same size as face of cube;
Centre left: Decal. Planar mapping icon larger than face of cube and slightly off-centre;
Centre right: Decal and Face. Planar mapping icon same size as face of cube;
Bottom: Tile. Tiling 3 × 3. Planar mapping icon same sizes as face of cube.

CHAPTER 8

Further rendering examples

Introduction

This chapter is intended as a revision of the contents of earlier chapters applied to examples which are more advanced than those already described, together with some notes on points to watch when creating 3D meshes and models for rendering in 3D Studio.

First example – 'space-ship'

The body of the 'space-ship' shown in Fig. 8.1 was constructed from two ellipses created in the **2D Shaper**, and lofted in the **3D Lofter** using one ellipse as a path and the second as a shape. After being **Object/ Made** in the **3D Lofter**, the mesh in the **3D Editor** was acted upon by **Modify/Object.../Skew** and **Modify/Object.../Bend** to its final shape. A hemisphere was then created in the editor and moved into position underneath the body. Ambient, Omni and Spot lights were included in the scene, all at maximum red colour. The material BLUE WIRE was assigned to the hemisphere. A camera with a focal length lens of 50 mm was added. A cloud background from SAMPLES/MAPS/ CLOUDS of the CD-ROM from Release 2 was included. The mesh and its lights, camera and background was then saved as a *.3ds mesh file

Fig. 8.1 Rendering of a 'space-ship', with a decal star pattern mapped on one side

Fig. 8.2 The shapes created
in the **2D Shaper** for the
star material

(SHIP.3DS) in order to allow a new material in the form of a star to be
made for adding as a decal material mapped onto the body of the
'space-ship'.

To make the material for the star, a reset was performed, clearing
all programs. Then the shapes shown in Fig. 8.2 were created in the
2D Shaper (press **F1**). **Shapes/Assign.../All** and **F3** pressed to get
back into the **3D Editor**, followed by **Create/Object.../Shaper** to
bring all the shapes already created into the **3D Editor** as a single
object. The material YELLOW PLSTC from the 3DS.MLI library
was assigned to the object and Ambient lighting set to full white
(255 in Red, Green and Blue), a camera added and the scene rendered
to examine the result. It appeared as in Fig. 8.3, with a star-shaped
hole into which the star was fitted and assigned the material BLUE
PLSTC.

A *right-click* brought back the **3D Editor** screen. **F1** was pressed to
bring back the **2D Shaper** and only the start shape assigned. **F3** was
pressed to get back to the editor and BLUE PLSTC assigned to the star.
A second rendering appeared – Fig. 8.3 – which was saved with **Anti-
Aliasing** and **Phong** shading as a file STAR.TGA – **Rendering/View.../
Save Last**.

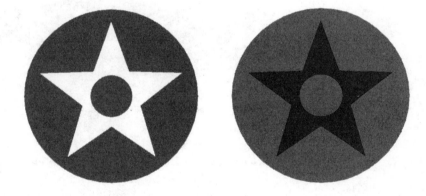

Fig. 8.3 The first and second
rendering of the star
material, showing the star-
shaped hole in the object
and a second material added
to the star

Making the star into a material

F5 was pressed to get into the **Materials Editor**. The file STAR.TGA
was loaded as a **Texture 1 map**. **Ambient**, **Diffuse** and **Specular**
lighting was set to white (255). The file was **Render**ed in a sampling
box with **Decal** highlighted (*left-click* on the button **S**) and saved as a
material in a new materials library file with the filename STAR
DECAL. A second rendering was made with **Tile** highlighted and the
tile material saved to the same library with a filename of STAR.TILE.

We now had two new materials – STAR DECAL and STAR TILE. The library in which the materials had been **Put** was then saved (**Library** pull-down menu). Note that if the directory to which you are saving a material library is not in your **Map Path**, a *left-click* on **Info** in the menu bar brings the **Info** pull-down menu. A *left-click* on **Configure** in the menu allows a **Map Path** to be added.

Mapping the star materials onto the 'space-ship'

The file SHIP.3DS was loaded into the **3D Editor**. A *left-click* on **Lights** and **Cameras** brought them back into the scene. From the saved library file **Surface/Choose.../Material** the material STAR DECAL was chosen. The material was assigned to the body of the space-ship and a planar map applied to a small surface of the body where the star was to appear. The resulting scene and the rendering is given in Fig. 8.1.

The material STAR TILE was assigned to the body of the space ship, the camera moved to a slightly better position and the scene again rendered. The result is shown in Fig. 8.4.

The STAR.TGA material can also be used as a background to a scene

Fig. 8.4 The rendering with STAR TILE mapped onto the body

as indicated in Fig. 8.5, by using **Rendering/Background** in the **3D Editor**. In the dialogue box which appears, choose STAR.TGA as the background material and the scene can then be rendered.

Second example – stained-glass window

This example (Fig. 8.6) follows on from the fourth example in Chapter 7 (page 117). A similar procedure was used, except that materials from the 3DS.MLI library were used instead of materials edited in the **Materials Editor**. Details of the shapes created in the **2D Shaper** for this example, together with the names of the materials assigned to the various shapes in the **3D Editor**, are given in Figure 8.7.

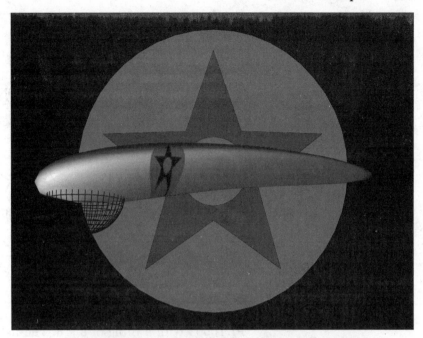

Fig. 8.5 STAR.TGA used as a background to a scene

Fig. 8.6 The rendering for the second Example

Third example – lamp

The rendering for this example is shown in Figure 8.9. The two parts of the lamp of this example were created in the **3D Editor** from two shapes created in the **2D Shaper** (Fig. 8.8). A flat surface was included on which the lamp stands. The lampstand was mapped with the material BRASS GIFMAP; the shade was mapped with the material

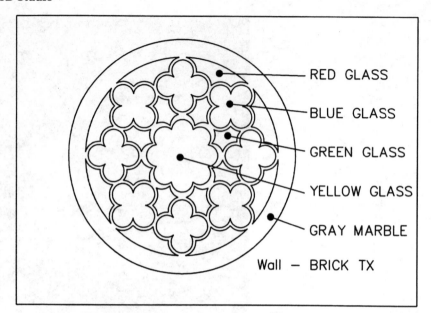

RED GLASS

BLUE GLASS

GREEN GLASS

YELLOW GLASS

GRAY MARBLE

Wall — BRICK TX

Fig. 8.7 Details of the shapes and the materials of the second example

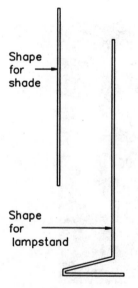

Shape for shade

Shape for lampstand

Fig. 8.8 The shapes from which the lampstand and its shade of the third example were created

PAT0003 with a tiling of 8 × 8. The flat surface was mapped with WOOD – DARK ASH. A single Spot light was placed inside the lamp-shade and set to produce a shadow. A white background was added to the scene with **Renderer/Setup.../Background**. In the **Background Method** dialogue box which appeared, the background colour was set

Fig. 8.9 The rendering for the third example

to 255 for all three colours – producing white. The rendering was with **Anti-aliasing** set and with **Shading** set to **Phong**.

Fourth example – table

This example was added to the third example. It was created in the **3D Editor** from shapes created in the **2D Shaper**. One leg was created and copied three times, then where necessary the copies were mirrored. After moving the legs to good positions in all three viewports – **Top**, **Front** and **Left** – a long rail was created and copied, followed by a short rail, also copied. The four rails were then moved to their final positions in the **3D Editor** and a top added with the aid of **Create/Box**. The mesh for the example is shown in Figure 8.10.

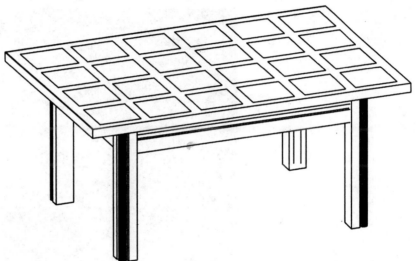

Fig. 8.10 The mesh for the fourth example

A new material, which was named TABFILE, was then created in the **Materials Editor** from the shapes shown in Figure 8.11. An outline surface for the table top (Figure 8.12) was created in the **2D Shaper** and taken into the **3D Editor**. This was followed by the shape of individual 'tiles' taken from the **2D Shaper** into the **3D Editor**, some of which were mapped with the material TABFILE. The remaining 'tiles' were assigned the material GOLD (LIGHT).

After adding a single Spot light above the table, setting Ambient light to a grey and adding a camera, the table was rendered – **Anti-aliasing** and **Phong** shading. The resulting rendering is shown in Figure 8.13.

Fifth example – room scene

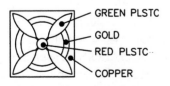

Fig. 8.11 The shapes for the new material TABFILE

This example is a combination of the third and the fourth. With the table mesh still in the **3D Editor**, the shapes for the lamp and its shade

Fig. 8.12 The shape for the tiled table top of the fourth example

Fig. 8.13 The rendered finish for the fourth example

were loaded back into the **2D Shaper**, taken into the **3D Lofter** and meshes made from **Path/SurfRev** paths. In the **3D Editor** the necessary materials and mapping were added to the shade and its stand.

Walls, a floor and skirting boards were added to the scene with the aid of **Create/Box**. The materials BUMPY WHITE STONE and PAT0003 were mapped onto the walls (tiling set at default of 1 × 1). The material LIGHT WOOD was mapped onto the floor with tiling set to X=1, Y=8. The skirtings had the material CREAM PLSTC assigned to their surfaces. An extra Spot light was included in the scene. Ambient lighting was set to 150 (Grey) and the scene rendered – Fig. 8.14.

Fig. 8.14 A rendering of the fifth example

Sixth example – Christmas decorations

This example – a rendering of a set of stars for Christmas decorations – was created from a DXF file from a drawing constructed in AutoCAD – Fig. 8.15. The drawing was constructed from a polyline outline, which in the User Coordinate System (UCS) of AutoCAD was copied twice and rotated 30° each side of the central vertical axis of the polyline. The triple polyline was then Polar arrayed twelve times around a central sphere. The sphere was constructed by Revsurfing a semicircle around its diameter. After saving the drawing as a DXF file, the DXF file was loaded into the **3D Editor**. The final rendering – Fig. 8.16 – was obtained as follows:

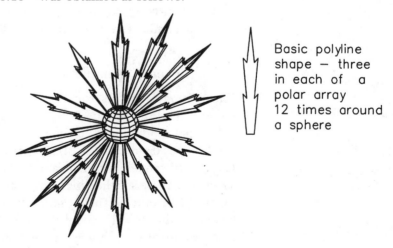

Basic polyline shape – three in each of a polar array 12 times around a sphere

Fig. 8.15 The AutoCAD drawing for the 3D model of the sixth example

Fig. 8.16 A rendering of the sixth example

1. In the **3D Editor**, the shape was copied four times to create five "stars". Ambient light was adjusted to give an overall gold colour light; two Spot lights were added, each set to a gold colour; a camera was added and adjusted to give suitable positions of the five stars in the Camera01 viewport.
2. The following materials were assigned to the stars: BRASS GIFMAP; CHROME BLUE SKY; CHROME GIFMAP; RED TILE PATTERN. The fifth star took its colouring from the gold colour of the lighting.
3. A background was selected from a *.CEL file from SAMPLES\MAPS on the CD-ROM disk from 3D Studio Release 2.
4. The scene was rendered (background: Anti-aliasing–High; Shading–Phong) and saved with a filename STARS.TGA.

Seventh example – kitchen layout

The 3D models for this example – a kitchen layout – could have been either taken from AutoCAD 3D drawings constructed with the aid of Advanced Modelling Extension (AME) or created in the **3D Editor** from shapes created in the **2D Shaper** and lofted in the **3D Lofter**. In fact the 3D models for the example were constructed in AutoCAD, saved as DXF files for loading into the **3D Editor**. The rendering shown in Fig. 8.19 is only part of the whole kitchen. Later in Chapter 11 it will be shown that the 3D models used for this Example can be used to create a form of walk-through scene. It should be noted here that all the models for this Example are of very simple construction. More fully realistic models could have been constructed, but they would have been beyond the scope of this book. The rendering (Fig. 8.19) resulted from the following sequence:

1. The walls, doors, doorways, window frame and floor of the kitchen were drawn in AutoCAD – Fig. 8.17. Each part of the drawing was constructed on its own named layer – walls on layer WALL; doors on layer DOORS; window on layer WINDOW and so on.

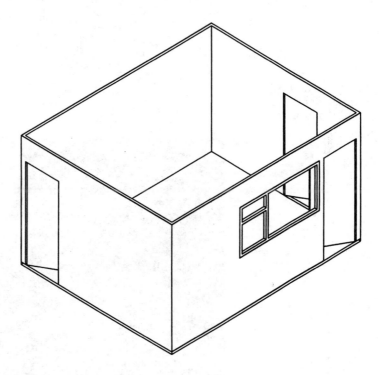

Fig. 8.17 The walls, doorways, doors, window frame and floor for the kitchen of the seventh example

2. A number of items of furniture and fittings for the kitchen were then constructed inside the kitchen walls – some of these are shown in Fig. 8.18. Many layers were used for these items – cupboards on layer CUPBOARD; cupboard doors on layer CUPDOOR; sink on layer SINK; worktops on layer WORKTOP and so on.
3. All items in the 3D drawing – kitchen and its fittings and furniture – were meshed with the AME command solmesh. The complete drawing was then saved as a DXF file.
4. The DXF file was loaded into the **3D Editor**. In the **Loading DXF File** dialogue box, **Derive objects from:** was set to **Layer** to enable each separate item from the DXF file to be loaded as a separate object in the **3D Editor** and then welded. Failure to observe this precaution would have resulted in a set of 3D meshes which would not have

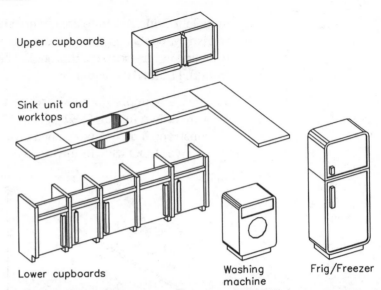

Upper cupboards

Sink unit and
worktops

Fig. 8.18 Some of the fittings
and furniture for the kitchen
of the seventh example

Lower cupboards

Washing
machine

Frig/Freezer

Fig. 8.19 A rendering of the
seventh example

been distinguishable from each other for assigning materials and
adding mapping.
5. Ambient light was set to 150; Two Spot lights were included, one
set to full white (255), the other to a greyish light (180).
6. A camera of focal length 50 mm was added and its position changed
to produce a good view in the Camera01 viewport.
7. Materials were assigned to each part:

Walls: GREEN MATTE.
Doors: WOOD MED ASH – mapped.
Floor: WOOD INLAY – A – mapped 12 × 12.
Worktops: WOOD WHITE ASH – mapped 12 × 1.
Cupboards: CREAM PLSTC.
Cupboard doors: GOLD.
Drawers: BLUE PLASTIC.
Sink and handles: CHROME GIFMAP – mapped.
Background: CLOUD02.TGA – SAMPLES\MAPS\CLOUDS – CD-ROM.

8. The scene was rendered with anti-aliasing off and Flat shading to give a quick rendering to check colours, materials, shadows and lights.
9. Finally the rendering parameters were changed to anti-aliasing high and Phong shading to obtain the final rendering. This was saved to the file name KITCHEN.TGA.

Eighth example – gear chain

The final example for this chapter is a rendering of a chain of three spur gears derived from an AutoCAD 3D solid model constructed using the Advanced Modelling Extension (AME) command set. The solid model was constructed from a polyline outline of three gear wheels, each then being acted upon by SOLEXT to change the 2D polyline outline into a 3D solid. The three gears (Fig. 8.20) were each constructed on their own separate layers and saved to a DXF file. The DXF file was loaded into the **3D Editor**. When loading the DXF file the **Layer** button of the **Derive objects from:** dialogue box was made active. The gears were then loaded as 3 objects. As loading continued, the following appeared at the Status line:

Loading DXF file, please wait followed by:
Loading DXF file: 1 objects, please wait followed by:
Loading DXF file: 2 objects, please wait followed by:
Loading DXF file: 3 objects, please wait

Fig. 8.20 The 3D mesh for the eighth example created with the aid of AME in AutoCAD and saved as a DXF file

When loaded, 2 Spot lights and a camera were added and the materials CHROME GIFMAP and BRASS GIFMAP were assigned and then mapped to the three objects (Fig. 8.21).

A white (255) background for the rendering was set and the rendering was with **Anti-aliasing** set and shading set to **Metal**.

Fig. 8.21 A rendering of the eighth example

Questions

1. Why is it important to ensure that when making a new material you determine whether it is to be a **decal** or a **tile** material?
2. If you get a set of four shapes, one inside the other, from the **2D Shaper** into the **3D Editor**, what would you expect to see if the four shapes were rendered?
3. What happens if you forget to map a material onto an object which has mapping parameters and then render the object?
4. In how many ways can a 3D mesh be loaded into the **3D Editor**?
5. Why is it important to watch what appears in the Status and Prompt lines when working in 3D Studio?
6. What will happen if you attempt rotating a planar mapping icon in a viewport without following its rotation angle in the Status line?
7. Why is it important to ensure that the directory path has been configured in the **Map Path** of the **Program Configuration** dialogue box, when loading your own library set of materials?
8. Why is it best not to interfere with the file 3DS.SET of the 3D Studio files unless you are the sole operator of the computer in use?
9. Why should repeated use be made of the **HOLD** and **FETCH** buttons of the Icon panel when working in 3D Studio?

10. When would you construct a 3D model in AutoCAD for rendering in 3D Studio rather than create the model in the programs of 3D Studio?

Exercises

Rather than set a number of exercises, the reader is advised to attempt rendering of objects somewhat like those shown in this chapter. It must, however, be borne in mind that unless you are a fairly experienced AutoCAD operator the last three examples will present some difficulty.

CHAPTER 9

Operating notes

Anti-aliasing

What appears on a computer screen is obtained by turning pixels on or off – they are lit or not lit. A screen with a high resolution has a greater number of pixels than one with a lower resolution. The **Materials Editor** screen of 3D Studio Release 2 has a resolution of 600 by 350 pixels. The other program screens may have higher resolutions, depending upon the type of monitor and the video driver used with the monitor. The illustrations in this book were created on a screen with a resolution of 800 by 600 pixels. One of the settings for rendering in 3D Studio is **Anti-aliasing** set in the **Render Still Image** dialogue box (Fig. 9.1). With no anti-aliasing, the edges of an area being rendered appear jagged, because no allowance is made for turning pixels on except those that are fully covered by the area being rendered. With **Anti-aliasing** set the software allows those pixels partly covered by the shaded area to be lit to an intensity comparable to the areas of the pixels which are partly covered by the rendered area. One drawback with anti-aliasing is that more memory is required, because of the complications of the mathematical formulae which allow for the intensity of individual pixels to be judged. Anti-aliasing will also take longer to perform. The difference between anti-aliasing off and anti-aliasing on is shown in a diagrammatic form in Fig. 9.2.

Fig. 9.1 Part of the **Rendering Still Image** dialogue box

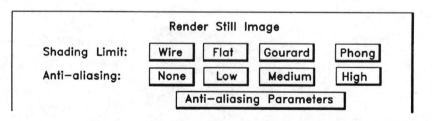

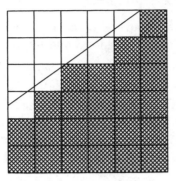

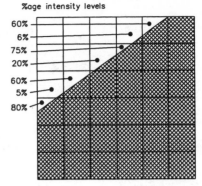

%age intensity levels

60%
6%
75%
20%
60%
5%
80%

Area rendered with anti—aliasing OFF

Area rendered with anti—aliasing HIGH

Fig. 9.2 A diagrammatic representation of anti-aliasing

Shading limits

Another of the settings to be made in the **Rendering Still Image** dialogue box is the **Shading Limit**. The four shading limits are **Force wire**, **Flat**, **Gouraud**, **Phong** and **Metal**. The differences resulting from four of these shadings are shown in Fig. 9.3. **Force wire** shading is of value to ascertain whether or not the objects in a scene are correctly positioned relative to each other. **Flat** shading, particularly if the **Anti-aliasing** is off, results in the rendering appearing fairly speedily. **Gouraud** (not illustrated here), **Phong** and **Metal** shading take longer, but if set with anti-aliasing, give the best shading results, with a considerably smoother appearance and with highlights showing. The titles of two of the forms of shading come from the names of their inventors – Henri Gouraud and Bui. T. Phong.

Fig. 9.3 **Force wire**, **Flat**, **Phong** and **Metal** shadings compared. Note that none of the materials assigned to the objects in the scene show in **Force wire** shading

Revision notes

1. There are several ways in which 3D meshes can be created in the **3D Editor** ready for rendering:

   (a) A 3D mesh can be created in the **3D Editor**.
   (b) A 3D mesh can be loaded into the **3D Editor** from a DXF file.
   (c) A 3D mesh can be obtained from a Shape created in the **2D Shaper** and lofted in the **3D Lofter**.
   (d) A 3D mesh can be or can include a shape taken directly from the **2D Shaper** into the **3D Editor**.

2. Always keep an eye on the Status and Prompt line. The first contains information about the positions of X, Y and Z coordinates and the movement of objects. The second gives the operator information about what their next operation should be.

3. When rotating an object, make sure you are keeping an eye on the degrees of rotation which appear in the Status bar as rotation proceeds. If rotation is to be clockwise the degree figure will have a minus sign (–) before its figures. For anti-clockwise rotation there will be no sign in front of the figures. It is only by *clicking* when the correct figure appears that exact rotation, say 90° or 45°, can be achieved. The figures appear in 0.25° intervals.

4. When in the **3D Editor** and using **Create/Object.../Get Shape**, the shape from the **2D Shaper** will appear in the current viewport. Make the viewport current (*left-click* within its area) in which you want the shape to appear before **Get Shape**. Failure to observe this precaution could well result in finding a shape in the wrong position relative to other parts of a 3D mesh.

5. When rendering a scene, it is advisable to check whether lighting and materials are satisfactory by making a first rendering with **Anti-aliasing** set off and shading set to **Flat**. This will give a much quicker rendering than with the higher settings. There is not a great deal of point in rendering to **Force wire** shading, except when you wish just to check the positions of features in a scene.

6. *Left-click* on **Info** in the Status bar, followed by a *left-click* on **Configure** in the pull-down menu – Figure 9.4. The **Program Configuration** dialogue box which appears – Figure 9.5 – shows the paths by which various files can be called. A second *left-click* in the **Map Paths** button brings up the **Specify Map Paths** dialogue box – Fig. 9.6. Paths for features such as *.tga files for backgrounds and *.mli libraries containing files of materials can be entered in this dialogue box if required. If a file in a directory not in the **Map Paths** is required, it will not load into 3D Studio.

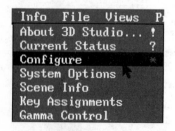

Fig. 9.4 The **Info** pull-down menu

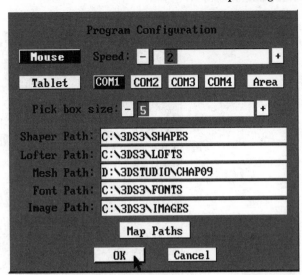

Fig. 9.5 The **Program Configuration** dialogue box

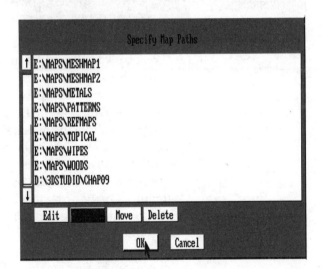

Fig. 9.6 The dialogue box appearing with a *left-click* on **Map Paths** in the **Configuration** dialogue box

7. Directory paths can be set so that they are always available when 3D Studio is operating. They can be specified in the **MAP-PATH** lines of the file 3DS.SET, which specifies parameters for the operation of 3D Studio. Fig. 9.7 shows that part of my 3DS.SET file dealing with **MAP-PATHS**. In the paths in this illustration it will be noted that several have been set to give access to the CD-ROM files from Release 2 – on my disk drive E:.

8. Do not make alterations to the 3DS.SET file unless you are the only operator of 3D Studio on the computer in use. Amending the file when other operators may be using the software could cause them inconvenience.

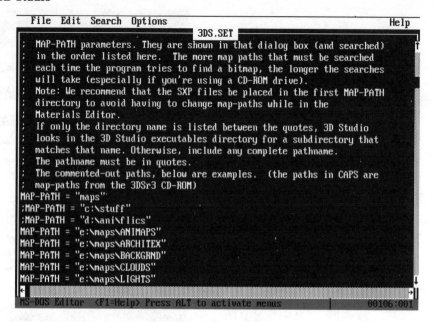

Fig. 9.7 The 3DS.SET file in the MS-DOS editor

9. Look back to Figure 8.3 (page 125). If several shapes such as the two in the star and its surround in that example are taken from the **2D Shaper** into the **3D Editor**, the spaces between the shapes will be holes, which in the example given has been filled with extra shapes to allow the materials to be assigned to shapes within the holes. However, once the holes have been filled, you may find difficulty in applying mapping to the shapes in the holes, because they may be difficult to pick. If this situation arises, some care is required in the order in which shapes are taken into the **3D Editor** for mapping to be applied.

10. It is often necessary to move objects in the programs of 3D Studio. Moving is an easy operation, but accuracy in moving can be increased by first making full use of Snap set to suitable unit sizes and the unidirectional cursor, which can be easily set to move horizontally, vertically or in any direction by toggling with the **Tab** key of the keyboard.

11. Other features which will greatly assist the operator in positioning with accuracy in the **3D Editor** are the Switch to full screen viewports and the Zoom buttons in the icon panel. The smallest possible area of any viewport other than a camera viewport can be examined with the aid of these two icons. If doubtful of complete accuracy, use Snap, the unidirectional cursor and both icons – Fig. 9.8.

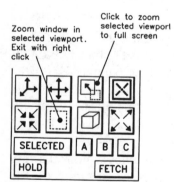

Zoom window in selected viewport. Exit with right click

Click to zoom selected viewport to full screen

Fig. 9.8 The **3D Editor** Icon panel

12. Also in the icon panel, remember to make frequent use of the **HOLD** and **FETCH** buttons, allowing each stage of your work to be

held in a buffer to be fetched from the buffer if an error is made after the **HOLD** button has been selected.

13. Mapping and the tiling of mapping – take care when making a material that you know quite clearly whether it is to be a **Decal** or **Tile** mapping material.

14. A command can always be stopped by pressing the **Esc** key of the keyboard. This cancels what has already been entered as part of a command and prompts start again for the current command.

15. Save your work at regular intervals. Get into the habit of saving at say every 15 minutes. Failure to observe this practice can result in the loss of work due to subsequent computer failure, electricity supply failure, etc.

16. There is a large number of warning, message and dialogue boxes associated with 3D Studio. Avoid the tendency to ignore some details in some of the boxes. The time spent in checking them will be saved by mistakes not occurring.

Keyboard entry for creating objects and shapes

In the 3D Editor

When creating objects in the **3D Editor** there are two main methods of determining the positions of corners, centres etc. and radius, height etc. The method used so far in this book has been by positioning the cursor hairs under the control of the mouse, followed by a *left-click* to determine the desired position, followed by two *left-clicks* within a viewport to determine the radius, height etc. Another method which is of particular value when wishing to construct to unit values or when positioning an object above or below the XY plane – i.e. in a Z-direction – is by entering coordinate numbers, radii and lengths of sizes at the keyboard.

When keyboard entry is possible a colon (:) appears after the prompt in the prompt line. The operator can then enter size figures at the keyboard in place of determining positions with the mouse.

Two examples of keyboard entry are given, one for the creation of a box object, the second for the creation of a cylinder. Remember we are working in three dimensions in the **3D Editor**, so in every case of coordinate entry from the keyboard an X, a Y and a Z coordinate figure will be required. After each coordinate figure has been entered at the keyboard the *Return* key of the keyboard must be pressed.

Example 1: Create/Box

In the Prompt line   **Place one corner of box:**   *Enter* 100 *Return*
In the Status line   **Box corner 1 X: 100 Y:**

In the Prompt line	**Place one corner of box:** *Enter* 100 *Return*
In the Status line	**Box corner 1 X: 100 Y: 100 Z:**

In the Prompt line	**Place one corner of box:** *Enter* 0 *Return*
In the Status line	**Box corner 2 X:**

In the Prompt line	**Place one corner of box:** *Enter* 200 *Return*
In the Status line	**Box corner 2 X: 200 Y:**

In the Prompt line	**Place one corner of box:** *Enter* 200 *Return*
In the Status line	**Box corner 2 X: 200 Y:**

In the Prompt line	**Place one corner of box:** *Enter* 100 *Return*

Fig. 9.9 The **Name for new object:** dialogue box

The **Name for new object:** dialogue box appears – Fig. 9.9. *Enter* a name if thought necessary, or adopt the **Object01** name and *left-click* on **OK**. Views of the box appear in all viewports.

Example 2: Create/Cylinder.../Smoothed

In the Prompt line	**Place center of 18-sided 1-segment cylinder:** *Enter* 0 *Return*
In the Status line	**X: 0 Y:**

In the Prompt line	**Place center of 18-sided 1-segment smoothed cylinder:** *Enter* 0 *Return*
In the Prompt line	**Place center of 18-sided 1-segment smoothed cylinder:**
In the Status line	**X: 0 Y: 0 Z** *Enter* 0 *Return*
In the Status line	**Radius:** *Enter* 100 *Return*
In the Status line	**Angle:** *Return*

In the Prompt line	**Click in viewport to define length of cylinder:** *Enter* 100 *Return*

The **Name for new object:** dialogue box appears. *Enter* a name, and *left-click* on **OK**. The cylinder will now appear in all of the viewports displayed on screen.

In the 2D Shaper

A similar system of keyboard entry is possible when creating shapes in the **2D Shaper**. The difference is, of course, that only two-dimensional shapes are possible, so only X and Y coordinate figures can be entered, there being no Z coordinate required. When a colon (:)

appears after a prompt, X and Y coordinate figures can be entered. As when entering coordinates in the **3D Editor**, the *Return* key must be pressed after entering either the X or the Y coordinate. The coordinate figures appear in the Status line as they are being entered.

Keyboard short-cuts

There are many key-stroke short-cuts available in 3D Studio. Only a selection of these will be given here. Keyboard short-cuts are indeed what they say. If used they will save a considerable amount of time when creating a complex scene. We have already seen the function key (those marked **F1**, **F2**, etc.) short-cuts to get into the four programs so far mentioned:

F1 for the **2D Shaper**.
F2 for the **3D Lofter**.
F3 for the **3D Editor**.
F5 for the **Materials Editor**.

Short-cuts associated with 3D Editor pull-down menus

Those shown here are from the **3D Editor** pull-down menus. In other programs the menus are slightly different, but will show the key-strokes against the command names in the menus. Note that the commands shown in black in the illustrations of the pull-down menus are commands not currently available – perhaps, for example, because there is nothing to save, there being nothing created on screen, the **Save** name is in black.

Shown in the **Info** pull-down menu – Fig. 9.4 (page 140):

Fig. 9.10 The **File** pull-down menu showing some other key-stroke short-cuts

!   brings up a message box with details about the software package.

?   brings the Current Status message box on screen.

*   brings the Configuration dialogue box on screen.

Shown in the **File** pull-down menu – Fig. 9.10:

Ctrl/L   brings up the **Load File:** dialogue box.
Ctrl/M   brings up the **File Merge:** dialogue box.
Ctrl/D   brings up the **Delete File:** dialogue box.
Q   brings up a message box asking the operator if he/she wishes to quit 3D Studio. *Enter* a **Y** and the program closes.
Ctrl\S   brings up the **Save File** dialogue box.

Fig. 9.11 The **Views** pull-down menu of the **3D Editor** showing key-stroke short-cuts

As shown in the **Views** pull-down menu – Fig. 9.11:

'	redraw – the current viewport only.
~	redraw all viewports.
Ctrl/V	brings up the **Viewports** dialogue box.
Ctrl/A	brings on the **Drawing Aids** dialogue box.
S	sets **Snap** in the current viewport – an **S** appears to the right of the program name.
G	sets the **Grid** in the current viewport.

Short-cuts for changing viewports

In the current viewport the viewing position can be changed by:

B	sets the viewport to show a bottom view.
D	disables the viewport.
F	sets the viewport to show a front view.
K	sets the viewport to show a back view.
L	sets the viewport to show a left view.
T	sets the viewport to show a top view.

In the current viewport:

C	changes to give a camera view.
W	toggles between a single viewport and full screen.
Z	allows zoom out.
Ctrl/Z	allows zoom in.

Note: The above lists the key-stroke short-cuts most likely to be used. There are others not given here.

Examples of models using keyboard short-cuts

Parts of the construction of these two examples are described in sequences using as many key-strokes and keyboard entries as possible. The reader will determine for him/herself whether keying information to construct shapes or meshes is preferable to always using the mouse. Probably most operators will find that a combination of the two methods is the best. In any case it is not possible to fully create shapes or meshes in 3D Studio without making considerable use of selection by mouse (or other selection device – e.g. a tablet and puck). Only parts of the constructions are given because describing every action required would not only take up considerable space in this book, but would become rather tedious for the reader. However, sufficient construction details are given to allow the reader to apply them to the remainder of the examples if it is desired to copy them as exercises.

First example – a chair

The shapes for this example were created completely in 3D Studio.

1. **F1**: Into **2D Shaper**.
2. **S** and **G**: Set Snap and Grid. **S** appears at top of command column.
3. **Modify/Axis.../Show**: Shows axis as black cross.
4. **Create/Quad**.
5. *Enter* –10 *Return*   200 *Return*
   Enter 10 *Return*   0 *Return*
   Quadrilateral shape 200×20 created.
6. **Ctrl/A**: Brings up **Snap Spacing:** dialogue box.
   Enter 72 in **Snap Spacing:** box.
7. **A**: Sets Angle snap to desired 72°. An **A** appears next to the **S** at the top of the command column.
8. **Modify/Polygon.../Rotate**.
9. Hold down **Shift** key, *left-click* on the quadrilateral and while holding down the **Shift** key move the mouse to the right. The shape is copied and rotated by 72°. Repeat until there are five of the quadrilateral shapes around the **Axis**.
10. **Shape/Assign/All**.
11. **F2**: Into the **3D Lofter**.

Once in the **3D Lofter** use the following sequence:

12. **Path/Steps:** Set steps in the **Path Steps** dialogue box to 0.
13. **Path/Move Vertex Tab**: until the unidirectional cursor is vertical. Adjust path to a height of 30.
14. **Shapes/Get.../Shaper**: All five quadrilaterals appear in the lofter.
15. **Shapes/Center**.
16. **Objects/Make**: *Enter* **stand** in the **Object Name:** box of the **Object Lofting Controls** dialogue box and a *left-click* on **Tween** and on **Create**.
17. **F3**: Into the **3D Editor** to check that the 3D mesh of the stand part of the chair is OK.
18. **A**: To turn off the **Angle Snap**.
19. **F1**: Into the **2D Shaper**.
20. **Create/Line:**
    Enter –160 *Return*   160 *Return*. Press *Escape* to exit command.
    Enter 160 *Return*   160 *Return*. Press *Escape* to exit command.
    Enter –180 *Return*   140 *Return*. Press *Escape* to exit command.
    Enter 180 *Return*   –110 *Return*. Press *Escape* to exit command.
    Enter 180 *Return*   140 *Return*. Press *Escape* to exit command.
    Enter 180 *Return*   –110 *Return*. Press *Escape* to exit command.

The top and the two side lines of the seat shape have now been drawn.

The sequence of actions continues as follows:

21. **Create/Arc:**
    Center of Arc: *Enter* −160 140 *Return.*
    Radius: *Enter* 20 *Return.*
    Start Angle: *Enter* 90 *Return.*
    End Angle: *Enter* 180 *Return.*
22. **Create/Arc:**
    Center of Arc: *Enter* 160 140 *Return.*
    Radius: *Enter* 20 *Return.*
    Start Angle: *Enter* 0 *Return.*
    End Angle: *Enter* 90 *Return.* Remember that arcs are created anticlockwise (ccw) and angle 0° is in the East direction (right).
23. The third arc – for the front of the seat – cannot be created by keyboard entry. It must therefore be created with the aid of the mouse.
24. **Shape/Assign:** *Left-click* on the seat shape.
25. **F2:** Into the **3D Lofter.**
26. **Shapes/Get.../Shaper.**
27. **Path/Move Vector:** Move vector until it is 50 tall.
28. **Objects/Make:** In the **Object Lofting Controls** dialogue box *enter* **seat** in the **Object Name:** box. *Left-click* on **Create.**
29. **F3:** Into the **3D Editor.**
30. **Modify/Object.../Move:** Move the seat to a good position.

All other parts of the chair are left to the reader to work out. The resulting rendered chair is given in Fig. 9.12.

Second example – a drink with an umbrella

This rendering was developed in two stages. The toy Japanese umbrella was constructed in AutoCAD, saved as a DXF file and then taken into the **3D Editor.** The glass and its contents were created in 3D Studio and 'added' to the scene. Part of the sequence was as follows:

1. **Ctrl/L:** Brings up the **Select a mesh file to load** dialogue box.
2. *Left-click* on the ***.DXF** button and from the file list box *double-left-click* on the filename given for the umbrella.
3. **F1:** Into the **2D Shaper.**
4. **G** and **S:** Sets Grid and Snap.
5. **Ctrl/A:** In the **Snap Spacing** dialogue box which appears, *enter* 2 in the **X:** Snap setting, followed by a *left-click* on **Y:** which sets both **Y:** and **Z:** to the same setting as **X:**

Fig. 9.12 The first example –
an office chair

6. **Modify/Axis.../Show:** Axis appears as a small cross.
7. **Create Line:**
   Enter 　0 *Return* 　–80 *Return.*
   Enter 　70 *Return* 　–80 *Return.*
   Enter 　70 *Return* 　–78 *Return.*
   Enter 　10 *Return* 　–70 *Return.*
   Enter 　10 *Return* 　30 *Return.*
   Enter 　70 *Return* 　50 *Return.*
   Enter 　70 *Return* 　200 *Return.*
   Enter 　68 *Return* 　200 *Return.*
   Enter 　68 *Return* 　52 *Return.*
   Enter 　6 *Return* 　8 *Return.*
   Enter 　6 *Return* 　–78 *Return.*
   Enter 　0 *Return* 　–78 *Return.*
   Enter 　0 *Return* 　80 *Return.*
8. **Shape/Assign/All.**
9. **F2:** Into the **3D Lofter**.
10. **S** and **G:** Set Snap and Grid.
11. **Shapes/Get.../Shaper**.
12. **Path/Step:** Set steps to 5.

13. **Path/SurfRev:** In the **Surface of Revolution** dialogue box:
    Diameter: *enter* 160.
    Degrees: *enter* 360.
    Vertices: *enter* 10.
    Left-click on **Create**.
14. **Shapes/Move**: Move shape so that its left hand edge is central to the path curve of the Helix circle.
15. **Objects/Make:** In the **Object Lofting Control** dialogue box *enter* **glass** in the **Object Name:** box, *left-click* on **Tween** and **Contour**.
16. **F3**: Into the **3D Editor**.
17. **Create/Cylinder.../Smoothed:** Create a cylinder to fit inside the glass.
18. **Modify/Objects.../Move** and **Modify/Object.../Rotate**: Move the umbrella to a suitable position in the glass.
19. Add lights, a camera and the materials BLUE GLASS (glass) and RED PLSTC (cylinder) and render the scene.

Fig. 9.13 is a rendering of the umbrella for the scene and Fig. 9.14 a rendering of the completed scene.

Fig. 9.13 A Japanese umbrella

Coordinate grid settings

A reasonable understanding of 3D coordinate geometry is necessary when creating models in 3D Studio. When creating shapes and meshes using keyboard entry of coordinates, it is advisable to make notes of the positioning of coordinates for your mesh. Remember that normally,

Fig. 9.14 The umbrella placed in a glass with a drink

unless you change it, the default values for X, Y and Z are the central point in each viewport – the origin coordinate (0,0,0). Coordinates to the left, below and behind the origin point are negative. You may wish to change these values by amending the settings for the grid in the **Snap Spacing:** dialogue box (Fig. 9.15). If the **Grid Extent Starts:** values are set at 0, then the bottom left hand corner of the grid will be the coordinate origin (0,0,0). X and Y coordinates will then all be positive in the grid and Z coordinates will all be positive vertically from the screen surface towards the operator.

Questions

1. Which settings of Shading and Anti-aliasing would you use when checking that a rendering will show the materials you have assigned to your model?
2. When would you render with the Anti-aliasing setting at **High**?
3. Why use the **Wire** Anti-aliasing setting?
4. In how many ways can a 3D mesh be loaded into the **3D Editor**?
5. Why is it necessary to look carefully at the Status line when rotating an object in the **3D Editor**?

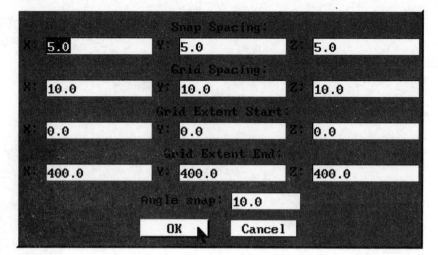

Fig. 9.15 The dialogue box for setting **Snap** and **Grid** showing values different to the default values

6. How do you set a path for background files found on the CD-ROM issued with 3D Studio?

7. What happens in the **3D Editor** when a shape consisting of a quadrilateral with two holes inside its outline is taken from the **2D Shaper** and rendered?

8. Which features can you use to ensure complete accuracy when moving objects in the **3D Editor**?

9. Which key-strokes are used for the following:
   To bring the **Snap Spacing:** dialogue box on screen?
   To set **Snap**?
   To set **Grid**?
   To load a 3D mesh?
   To switch into the **3D Lofter**?
   To change a viewport to a camera view?

10. How can the coordinate origin (0,0,0) be changed so as to be at the bottom left-hand corner of the grid pattern?

Exercises

The exercises below allow the copying of the renderings given in this chapter. Only the outlines of the drawings from which the 3D meshes were obtained are given. Sizes and other information not included are left to the reader's own judgment.

1. Fig. 9.16 shows the 3D mesh from which the renderings of Fig. 9.3 were obtained. The eyes and mouth were mapped onto the face from a material created in the **Materials Editor** which was made from a rendering of the shapes included in Fig. 9.16.

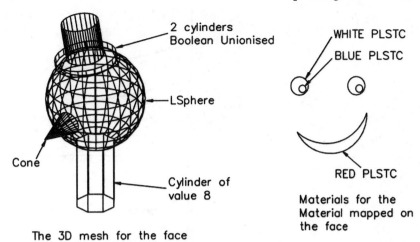

2 cylinders
Boolean Unionised

WHITE PLSTC

BLUE PLSTC

LSphere

RED PLSTC

Cone

Cylinder of
value 8

Materials for the
Material mapped on
the face

The 3D mesh for the face

Fig. 9.16 Exercise 1

2. Only the end view of the 3D mesh of the chair from which the rendering of Fig. 9.12 was obtained is given in Fig. 9.17. Other details are included with the description for constructing Example 1, starting on page 143.

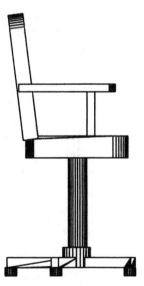

Fig. 9.17 Exercise 2

3. The rendering of the umbrella given in Fig. 9.13 was made from a 3D mesh created from a DXF file of an AutoCAD drawing. The outlines from which the Polar Arrays for the drawing in AutoCAD were obtained are given in Fig. 9.18. The 'waxed paper' for the umbrella covering had a new material made in the **Materials Editor** from shapes created in the **2D Shaper** and rendered from the **3D Editor**. The new material was tile mapped onto the 'waxed paper' mesh.

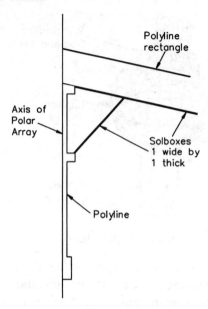

Fig. 9.18 Exercise 3

4. Details of the shape from which the wine glass rendering (Fig. 9.14) was created along a SurfRev path are given in Fig. 9.19. The 'wine' in the glass was a cylinder assigned the material RED NEON.

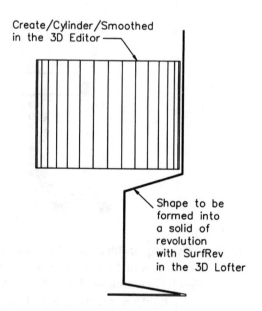

Fig. 9.19 Exercise 4

CHAPTER 10

Projects and Help

Introduction

A *left-click* on **File** in the menu bar brings the **File** pull-down menu on screen – Fig. 10.1. Several of the commands in this menu are concerned with Loading, Merging and Saving projects. When a scene is saved as a project file, everything included in the scene as well as data from all the 3D Studio programs is recorded:

Grid and **Snap** settings.
All 3D meshes.
All lights, cameras, materials and mappings.
Any shapes in the **2D Shaper**.
Any lofts in the **3D Lofter**.
The parameters for any materials created or edited in the **Materials Editor**.
All keys etc. in the **Keyframer** (see Chapter 11) if it has been used.

Fig. 10.1 **Load Project** from the **File** pull-down menu

A project file is saved with a file extension of ***.prj**. The value of project files is that they can be repeatedly re-loaded to be used as a lighting and camera set-up, as backgrounds for scenes, or for any other purpose where all details connected with a scene need to be used repeatedly. Two examples are given here – the first a simple lights and camera set-up which will allow any 3D models to be created within the lighting and camera of the project. The second is a more complicated project scene which forms a setting for furniture and fittings to be included in a room setting. Additional projects – e.g. a chair, a table, items of crockery and cutlery – could be saved as project files and recalled to be added to a project and merged with the background scene.

First example

Grid: Set to **X, Y, Z** 10,10,10 and on.
Snap: Set to **X, Y, Z** 5,5,5.

The settings for four lights within the project are:

Ambient: set at **RGB** 60,60,60.

Omni: A single light central to the scene.

Spot lights: Two spot lights from each front side of the position where 3D objects will be created. The right hand light was set to **RGB** 255,255,255. The second spot light was set to **RGB** 150,150,150.

A single camera near one of the spotlights is included.

The screen was then saved as a project file with the filename **ay.prj** – my initials followed by the .prj extension.

When required the project file can be selected from a **Select a Project file to load** dialogue box – Fig. 10.2. All settings then appear in the viewports.

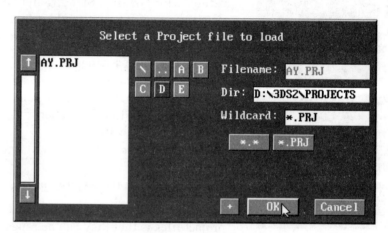

Fig. 10.2 The **Select a Project file to load** dialogue box

Fig. 10.3 shows the project file features for the first example before being saved.

Note: Project files are saved to a directory, usually named 3ds3\projects. This directory is specified in the 3ds.set file in which the parameters within which 3D Studio works are specified – directories for meshes, for shapes, for lofts etc. One of the lines in the 3ds.set file will be **PROJECT – 'projects'** showing that the directory in which projects files will be saved is 3ds3\projects. Associated with the directory are the dialogue boxes **Save a Project file** and **Select a Project file to load**.

Second example

The second example is more complicated as can be seen from the **3D Editor** screen of the project before it was saved to the file name

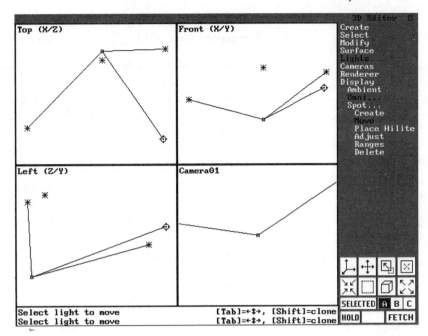

Fig. 10.3 The first example of a project set-up

room.prj – Fig. 10.4. The scene is based on the four walls of a room, with two windows, two doors, a floor and a ceiling, created directly from shapes, themselves created in the **2D Shaper**.

Two **Omni** lights were added, **Ambient** lighting was set to **RGB** 50,50,50 and a camera was included in the scene. The following

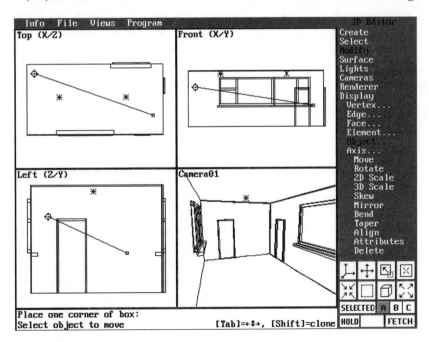

Fig. 10.4 The scene for the project room.prj

materials were assigned to the various parts of the meshes with a variety of mappings applied to the various parts of the scene:

Ceiling: The material WHITE PLSTC BMP from 3ds.lib was mapped without tiling.

Floor: The material CARPET.TGA from the CD-ROM with Release 2 was taken into the **Materials Editor**, given full **Ambient**, **Diffuse** and **Specular** white lighting, rendered and then saved as a new material FLOOR to my own library (book.mli). Mapping was **X**: 12, **Y**: 12.

End walls: The material PAT0011.TGA from the CD-ROM with Release 2 was taken into the **Materials Editor**, given full **Ambient**, **Diffuse** and **Specular** white lighting, rendered and then saved as a new material END WALLS to my own library (book.mli). Mapping was **X**: 10, **Y**: 10.

Long walls: The material FABRIC1.TGA from the CD-ROM with Release 2 was taken into the **Materials Editor**, given full **Ambient**, **Diffuse** and **Specular** white lighting, rendered and then saved as a new material LONG WALLS to my own library (book.mli). Mapping was **X**: 1, **Y**: 10.

Doors: The material WOOD-ASH from 3ds.mli was mapped onto the doors with **X**: 10, **Y**: 1.

Door and window surrounds: The material WHITE PLSTC from the 3ds.mli was assigned without mapping.

Renderer/Setup.../Background: background was taken from CLOUD6.TGA from the CD-ROM of Release 2.

Camera: was set with 50 mm lens for a first of two renderings – Fig. 10.5 and to 20 mm for the second rendering – Fig. 10.6.

The project was then used as a background to a number of furnished scenes from different camera settings and positions. These are not illustrated here.

Merge Project

Fig. 10.7 shows the dialogue box **Merge:** which appears when **Merge Project** is selected from the **File** pull-down menu. As can be seen, features within a merging project can be included or not included by selection from the buttons within the dialogue box. It is possibly unlikely that you would wish to duplicate the lighting or the camera already within the scene, so you will probably *left-click* on each of the buttons in turn to turn the lighting and cameras off in the merging project. The **Animation** button will also often be turned off. A *left-click* on **OK** and a second dialogue box appears – Fig. 10.8 – which shows that for the ROOM.PRJ being merged with another project. Selection

Fig. 10.5 The first of two renderings of the project scene room.prj with the camera lens set at 50 mm

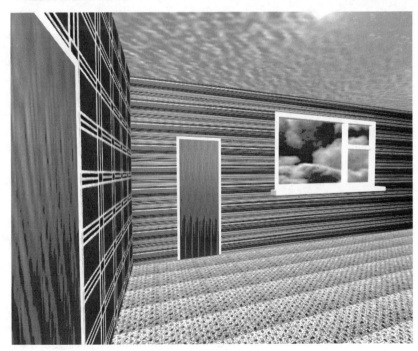

Fig. 10.6 The second of the two renderings of the scene room.prj taken from a different camera viewpoint and with the lens set at 20 mm

Fig. 10.7 The **Merge** pull-down menu which appears when **Merge** is selected from the **File** pull-down menu

Fig. 10.8 The **Select Objects to Merge** dialogue box

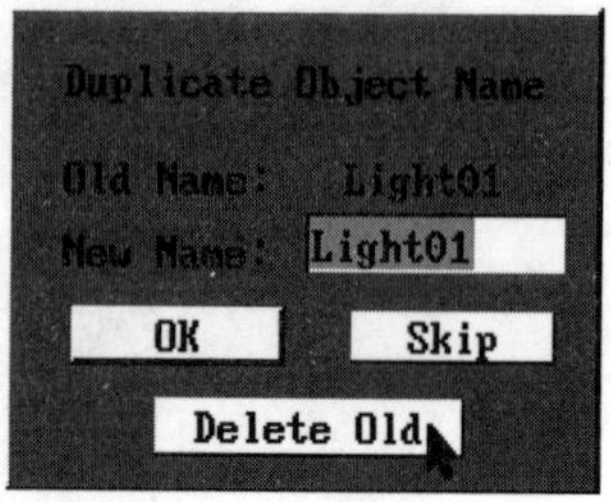

Fig. 10.9 The **Duplicate Object Name** dialogue box

of objects from the dialogue box can be made. If an object with a name the same as one of the objects already in a scene on screen appears in the project to be merged, yet another dialogue box appears – Fig. 10.9 – the **Duplicate Object Name** box. Either delete the old object by a *left-click* on **OK** or enter a new name in the **New Name:** box of the dialogue box. It will be seen from Fig. 10.9 that not only objects created in the project on screen may have to be re-named or deleted, but also lights, cameras etc.

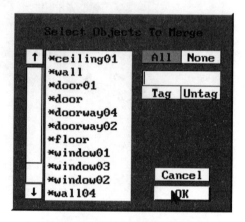

Notes

1. When merging another project file with that already on screen, it may be necessary to scale (**Modify/Object.../3DScale**) or move (**Modify/Object.../Move**) in order that the merged objects fit in the existing scene to good advantage.
2. If several objects make up the scene being merged, each object may have to be scaled or moved independently. If this happens, watch the Status bar carefully to ensure that scaling and/or moving is carried out to the same percentage scale or units moved for each of the modified objects.
3. When saving a rendered drawing, if the software loaded in the computer in use contains a compression facility, the file may be

saved in a compressed condition. This is a useful facility because many rendered files are large. For example, that of the rendered room project which was rendered to a file name room.tga, was 1.3 Mbytes in size. Compression of the file would have saved much disk space. This is the reason for the **Archive** command in the **File** pull-down menu (Fig. 10.1). But take care when archiving that your procedures are correct – the file may be lost if good procedures are not followed.

Help

Fig. 10.10 The cursor arrow and question mark associated with **Help**

If help is required for any command you are wishing to use in 3D Studio, press and hold down the **Alt** key of the keyboard. The cursor changes from an arrow to an arrow with a question mark besides it – Fig. 10.10. Move this cursor under control of the mouse over the command – which can be any item in any pull-down menu or any command showing yellow in the command column. *Left-click* on the command and a message box appears. An example is given in Fig. 10.11. A *left-click* on the **Continue** button in the message box or a *right-click* anywhere on screen and the box with its help message disappears.

Fig. 10.11 The **Help** message box associated with **Merge Project**

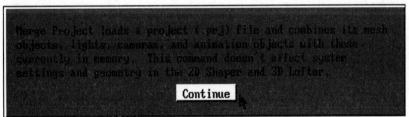

Merge Project loads a project (.prj) file and combines its mesh objects, lights, cameras, and animation objects with those currently in memory. This command doesn't affect system settings and geometry in the 2D Shaper and 3D Lofter.

Continue

Questions

1. What are the differences between a mesh file (extension *.3ds) and a project file (extension *.prj)?
2. What is the purpose of creating a project file?
3. What is the purpose of the command **Merge Project**?
4. What is the purpose of the **Duplicate Object Name** dialogue box?
5. When would you use the command **Archive** from the **File** menu?
6. How can help be called for a command?
7. Which commands have **Help** message boxes?

Exercises

1. Make up your own project file which contains your own lighting and camera settings.

2. Create a room scene similar to one of the rooms in your own home and then save it as a project file.
3. Create a number of items of furniture, save each one as a project file and then merge them with your room scene project.
4. Practise obtaining help from commands in the pull-down menus of each program and also for those commands which appear in yellow in the command columns of the programs.

CHAPTER 11

The Keyframer program

Introduction

The **Keyframer** program is used for the creation of animations. Each animation is made up of a number of frames (the parameters of which are known as keys), each of which can be rendered in sequence. The rendered frames can then be run and when viewed on the computer display screen, the sequence of rendered frames appear as if the keys within them are animated. Setting the parameters for the frames in the **Keyframer** program can be a complicated process and only the most elementary of examples are offered in this chapter. As with other details throughout this book, it is hoped that the introductory examples given in this chapter will encourage the reader to research and experiment in order to gain a good expertise in animating his/her 3D models in 3D Studio. When first opened – by selection from the **File**

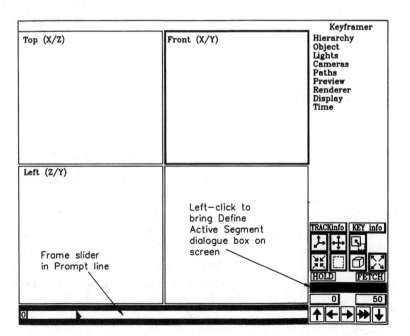

Fig. 11.1 The **Keyframer** program screen

pull-down menu, or by pressing the **F4** key, the screen appears as in Fig. 11.1. Note the similarities to the **3D Editor** screen – four viewports showing **Top**, **Front**, **Left** and **User** viewports. Also note the differences in the icon panel – Fig. 11.2.

Only the sequences for creating the animations of the three examples are given in this chapter:

1. The animation of a piston movement within its cylinder, the cylinder being in half section in order to display the movement in full.
2. An extension of the first example, with the addition of a revolving crank attached to a link which drives the piston.
3. A walk-through the kitchen scene created in an earlier chapter (page 156).

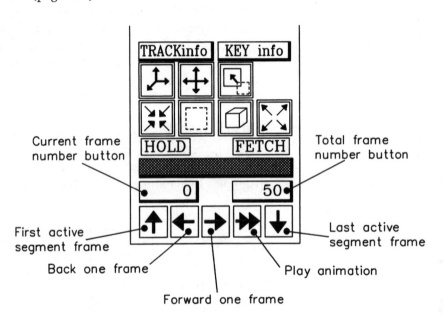

Fig. 11.2 The icon panel of the **Keyframer** program

First example – piston

1. Create the 3D mesh for the scene in the **3D Editor** as shown in Fig. 11.3. The mesh consists of two parts – the piston and the half cylinder. The piston is a Boolean Union of two cylinders, from which a third cylinder is Boolean Subtracted to form the hole and two parts Boolean Subtracted from the piston to form the cut-away at one end. The half cylinder is formed from Shapes created in the **2D Shaper** and lofted in the **3D Lofter** and then Boolean Unioned.
2. Two omni lights are added in the scene. Ambient light is set to 60/60/60.

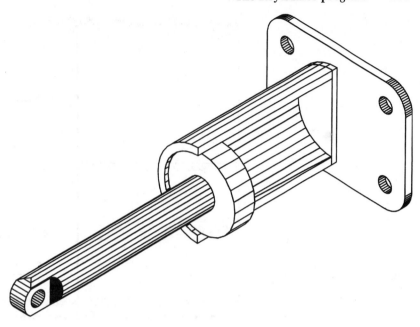

Fig. 11.3 The 3D mesh for
the first example

3. A camera is included in the scene.
4. **F4** into the **Keyframer** program.
5. *Left-click* on the **Define Active Segment** button (Fig. 11.1) and *enter* 50 in the **End:** box of the dialogue box Fig. 11.4. The same can be achieved by a *left-click* on the Total frame number button in the Icon panel and *entering* 50 in the **Set Number of Frames** dialogue box (Fig. 11.2). The screen will then appear as in Fig. 11.5.

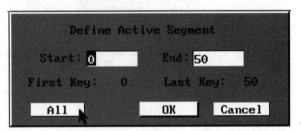

Fig. 11.4 The **Define Active Segment** dialogue box

6. Move the cursor under mouse control into the Prompt line and the Frame slider appears (Fig. 11.1). Drag the button labelled 0 until the number in the button is 25. Note that the colour of all objects in the viewports changes to black.
7. **Object/Move** and in the **Front (X/Y)** viewport press **Tab** until the unidirectional cursor is pointing horizontally.
8. Move the piston until it is almost at the extent of its stroke inside the half cylinder. Note that the piston changes colour to white after the move.

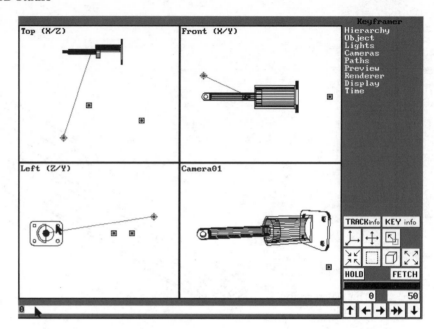

Fig. 11.5 The **Keyframer** screen after the various settings for the first example have been made

9. *Left-click* on the **TRACK info** button in the Icon panel. The **Track Info:** dialogue box appears – Fig. 11.6.

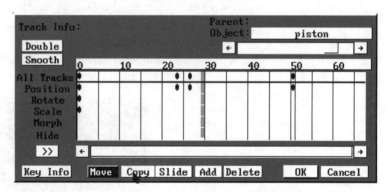

Fig. 11.6 The **Track Info:** dialogue box

10. In the dialogue box *left-click* on the **Move** button. Move the **Position** key from 25 to 21 – *left-click* on the key and drag it to 21 holding the mouse key down.

11. *Left-click* on the **Copy** button and copy the key at 21 to the 29 position.

12. While still in the **Track Info:** dialogue box *left-click* on the **Key Info** button. The **Key Info:** dialogue box appears – Fig. 11.7.

13. Set the number in **Key#** to 2 and adjust the **Ease To** slider to 25. Note the changes in the graph.

14. Set the **Key#** number to 3 and adjust the **Ease From** slider to 25. Again note the changes in the graph.

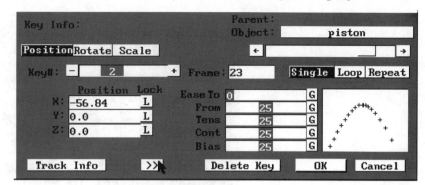

Fig. 11.7 The **Key Info:** dialogue box

15. *Left-click* on the play-back button (that with two arrows) to check whether the animation looks OK.
16. *Left-click* on **OK** in the dialogue box.
17. *Left-click* in the **Camera01** viewport to make it active.
18. **Renderer/Render View** and *left-click* in the **Camera01** viewport.
19. In the **Render animation** dialogue box, check that the **Disk** button is active (highlighted red), followed by a *left-click* on the **Render** button.
20. In the **Save rendered animation to file** dialogue box which appears (Fig. 11.8), *enter* a suitable file name in the **Filename:** box. *Left-click* on **OK**.

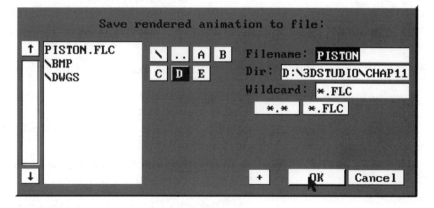

Fig. 11.8 The **Save rendered animation to file** dialogue box

21. Details of the rendering will be seen in the **Rendering in progress...** dialogue box (Fig. 11.9).

Notes

1. Materials and mapping can be added to an animation – in the **3D Editor** before changing over to the **Keyframer** program.
2. **Preview/Play** to see the animation.
3. But – **Rendered/View.../Image** and select the required ***.FLC** file

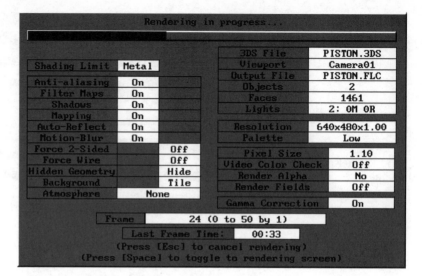

Fig. 11.9 The **Rendering in progress...** dialogue box during rendering

from the **View Image** dialogue box if the full animation complete with materials assigned in the **3D Editor** is required.

4. Rendering of an animation can take a considerable time because each segment will have to be rendered in turn. The examples given here take about 30 to 50 minutes for the renderings to be completed (working with a computer running at 66 MHz). More complicated animations may have to be left to render overnight or while work at another computer is proceeding.

Second example – linked piston and crank

This uses the same 3D mesh as the first example with the addition of a crank pivoted centrally to a backplate and connected to a link which operates the piston as the crank rotates through 360°. Fig. 11.10 shows the 3D mesh for this example.

The method of constructing the segments necessary to complete this animation follow the sequence:

1. In the **3D Editor** create the backplate and the link – Fig. 11.10.
2. Press **F4** into the **Keyframer**.
3. *Left-click* on the red strip button in the icon panel and in the **Define Active Segment** dialogue box which appears. *Enter* 50 in the **End:** box.
4. In the prompt line drag the number button to the right hand end of the slider to read 50.
5. **Hierarchy/Object Pivot**. *Left-click* on the crank in the **Front (X/Y)** viewport and place the pivot (a small black cross) at the centre of the pivot at the left-hand end of the crank.

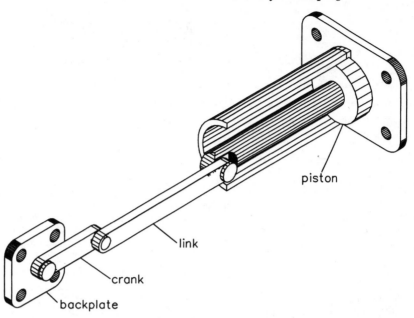

piston

link

crank

backplate

Fig. 11.10 The 3D mesh for the second example

6. **Object/Rotate**. *Left-click* on the crank and rotate it through 360° anti-clockwise, following the rotation in degrees in the Status bar. Note that the crank rotates about the pivot set by **Object/Pivot**.

7. *Left-click* on the **Key info** button in the Icon panel. **Copy** the keys from 0 to 50 for the crank, link and piston.

8. **Hierarchy/Link**:
   In the prompt line: **Select child of object:** *left-click* on the link.
   In the prompt line: **'Link' selected. Now select parent of link:** *left-click* on the crank. See **Note** below.

9. In the Prompt line, drag the number button to 5. The Crank will be seen rotated through 36°, with its child (the link) rotated with it.

10. **Hierarchy/Object Pivot** and set a pivot at the left hand pivot point in the link.

11. **Object/Rotate** and rotate the link around its pivot until its right hand end lines up with the centre line of the piston. Note that the parent of the link (the crank) does not rotate with the link.

12. **Object/Move**. *Left-click* on the piston and move it horizontally until the pivot at its left hand end coincides with the pivot at the right hand end of the link. See Fig. 11.11 and Fig. 11.12. Use the Tab key to set the uni-directional cursor in its horizontal position for this move.

13. Repeat **12** at segments 10, 15, 20, 25, 30, 35, 40 and 45, rotating the link and moving the piston each time. Fig. 11.11 shows the positions of the three objects after rotating the link and moving the piston at segments 0, 5, 10 and 15. Figs 11.12 and 11.13 show the three

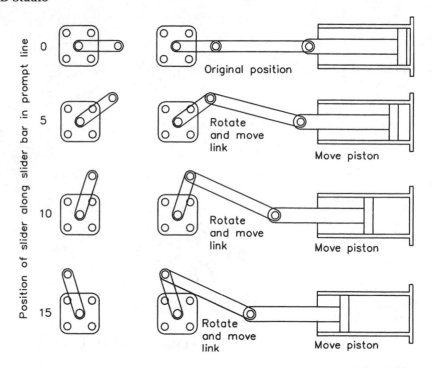

Fig. 11.11 Positions of the crank, link and piston after each fifth key position - 0, 5, 10 and 15

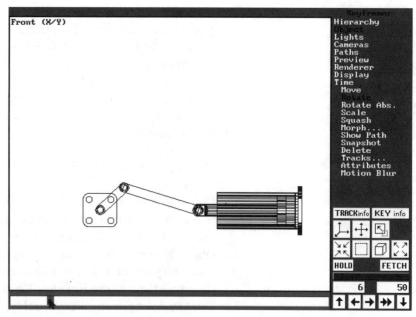

Fig. 11.12 The crank, link and piston showing in the **Front (X/Y)** viewport in segment 5 after rotating the link and moving the piston

objects at segment 5 and segment 18 in the **Front (X/Y)** viewport, and Fig. 11.14 shows a rendering of the scene at segment 10.

14. Drag the number button in the prompt line through its whole range from 0 to 50. At positions where the crank, link and piston appear

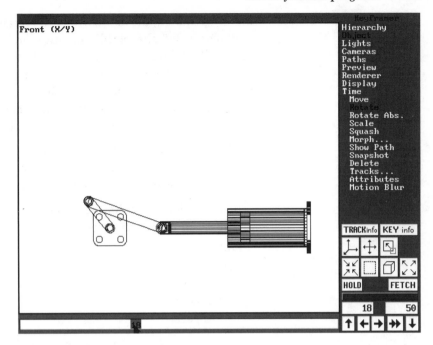

Fig. 11.13 The crank, link and piston showing in the **Front (X/Y)** viewport in segment 18 after rotating the link and moving the piston

Fig. 11.14 A rendering of the scene at the 10th segment

to be in wrong positions relative to each other, some adjustments may be necessary.

15. **Preview/Play** to see the animation running.
16. **Renderer/View** and *left-click* in the **Camera01** viewport and render to the screen and to disk as in the First Example.
17. When the rendering is completed (about 50 minutes on my computer) play back the flic file which has been saved to disk.

Notes

The hierarchical linking parent/child is an important feature of animations in 3D Studio. A further instance of this linking is given in the third example. A 'parent' is linked to a 'child' in a 'family'. If the 'parent' moves, the 'child' must go with the 'parent', but the 'child' can move on its own. In the example just given, when the 'parent' (the crank) is rotated, the 'child' (the link) rotates with it. However, at the end of each 36°, the 'child' (the link) can be rotated independently of the crank. A hierarchy of parent/child relationships can be built up throughout a scene which is to be animated. This relationship will show in a dialogue box – the **Object Attachment Tree** box when **Hierarchy/Show Tree** is selected – an example of which is given in Fig. 11.17. Taking as an example the human body:

The fingers are children of its parent (the hand).
The hand is a child of its parent (the lower arm).
The lower arm is a child of its parent (the upper arm) and so on.

In an **Object Attachment Tree** dialogue box, this parent/child relationship would show as:

body*
 upper arm*
  lower arm*
   hand*
    finger*

In this tree, when the body is moved, the upper arm, the lower arm, the hand and the finger will also move.
When the upper arm is moved, the lower arm, the hand and the finger will move, but the body will not.
When the lower arm is moved, the hand and finger move, but the upper arm and the body do not, and so on.
When the finger is moved, it is only the finger that moves.

Third example – weather vane

In this example a small family tree is created, in which a set of 12 vanes (the object **vane12**) rotates as a 'child' of a 'parent' stand (the object **stand01**), while the stand is a 'child' of a 'parent' base (the object **base**). Due to creation of the hierarchical 'family', the vanes rotate around their pivot as the stand with the rotating vanes circles around the circumference of the base.

Fig. 11.15 shows the 3D mesh from which this animation originates. The object **vane12** is constructed from an ellipse created in the **2D Shaper** and lofted through 1.5 units in the **3D Lofter**, rotated in plan by 10° and then arrayed around a central cylinder 12 times before being formed into a single Boolean Union by **Create/Object . . . Boolean**. The object **stand01** is a cylinder to which a smaller cylinder has been Boolean unioned. The object **vane12** pivots on the smaller cylinder. The base is a cylinder of height 15 units.

The animation was created in the sequence:

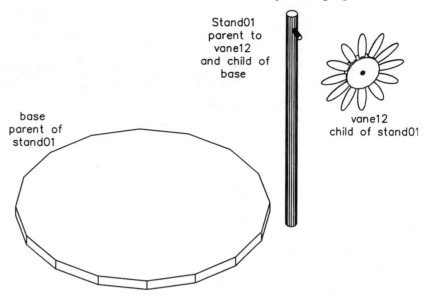

Stand01
parent to
vane12
and child of
base

vane12
child of stand01

base
parent of
stand01

Fig. 11.15 The 3D mesh for
the third example

1. Create the 3D mesh in the **2D Shaper, 3D Lofter** and **3D Editor**.
2. Add lights and a camera.
3. Press **F4** and into the **Keyframer** – Fig. 11.16.

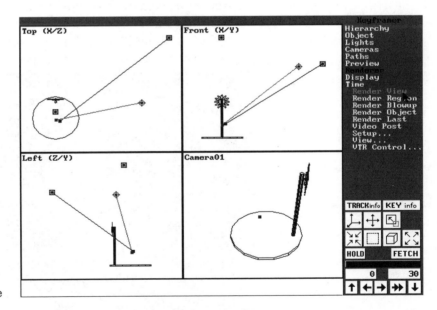

Fig. 11.16 The **Keyframer**
screen for the third example

4. **Hierarchy/Link**. *Left-click* on the object **vane12**, followed by a *left-click* on the object **stand01**. **Vane12** then becomes the 'child' of its 'parent' **stand01**.
5. *Left-click* on **stand01**, followed by a *left-click* on **base**. This makes **stand01** the 'child' of the 'parent' **base**.

6. **Hierarchy/Show Tree**. The **Object Attachment Tree** dialogue box for the scene – Fig. 11.17 – appears.

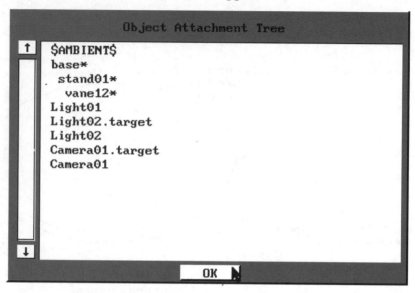

Fig. 11.17 The **Object Attachment Tree** dialogue box for the third example

7. *Left-click* on the button in the icon panel to bring up the **Define Active Segment** dialogue box to check that the last segment is 30.
8. Drag the number box in the prompt line until it reads 30.
9. *Left-click* in the **Front (X/Y)** viewport to make it active. **Object/ Rotate** and rotate **vane12** clockwise through 720°.

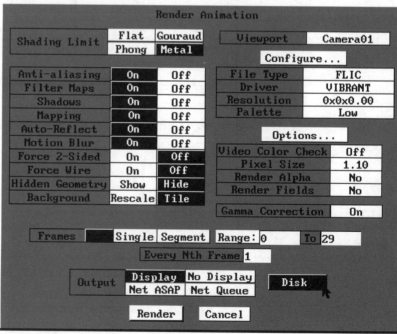

Fig. 11.18 The **Render animation** dialogue box for the third example

10. *Left-click* in the **Top (X/Z)** viewport to make it active. **Object/ Rotate** and rotate **stand01** anti-clockwise through 360°.

11. **F3** into the **3D Editor** and add materials and mapping to the three objects in the scene. Adjust the rendering background to a light grey.

12. **Preview/Play** to check that the animation works well.

13. **F4** into the **Keyframer. Renderer/View** and render the **Camera01** viewport.

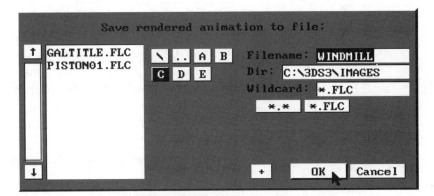

Fig. 11.19 The **Save rendered animation to file?** dialogue box for the third example

Fig. 11.20 A rendering of one position in the animation of the third example

14. Make the **Disk** button active in the **Render animation** dialogue box – Fig. 11.18 – and enter a suitable file name in the **Filename:** box of the **Save rendered animation to file?** dialogue box, followed by a *left-click* on **OK** – Fig. 11.19. The rendering took about 30 minutes on my computer.

15. Fig. 11.20 shows a rendering of the third example at one stage in the animation.

Fourth example – room walk-around

This example demonstrates how the **Keyframer** program can be used to create an animation representing a walk-around in a room. The 3D mesh from which the animation was created was derived from a project file described in Chapter 10 (page 156). In order to construct such an animation a path is built for the camera to follow and the animation becomes a series of renderings of the camera positions along the path.

The procedure for developing the animation follows the sequence:

1. In the **Keyframer** program, *left-click* on **File** in the menu bar, followed by a *left-click* on **Load Project** and a *double-left-click* on ROOM.PRJ in the **Select a Project file to load** dialogue box.

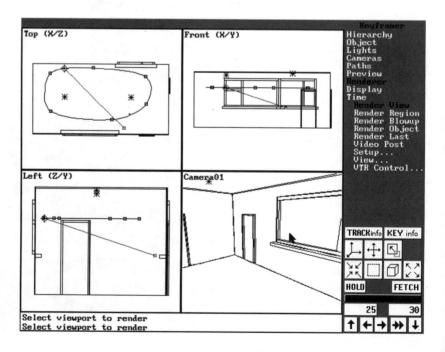

Fig. 11.21 The **Keyframer** screen after the **Path** for the camera has been created

2. Move the number box in the prompt line to 5.
3. **Cameras/Move**. *Left-click* on the camera in the **Top (X/Y)** viewport and move the camera to a new position.
4. Repeat **3** at positions 10, 15, 20 and 25, moving the camera positions at each segment to form a loop, somewhat like an ellipse in shape.
5. *Left-click* on the **Track info** button in the Icon panel. **Copy** the keys from the 0 segment to the 30 segment.
6. **Cameras/Show Path**. *Left-click* on the camera in the **Front (X/Y)** viewport. The camera path appears, linking the positions of the camera in the segments 5 to 30 by a red broken line.
7. **Paths/Move Key**. *Left-click* on each key in the path in turn and move each key to a more suitable position to form a fairly regular curve – Figures 11.21 and 11.22.
8. *Left-click* on the play-back arrows in the Icon panel to check that the animation works reasonably well.
9. **Renderer/Render View**. *Left-click* in the **Camera01** viewport and render the animation. The 30 renderings took about 90 minutes on my computer.

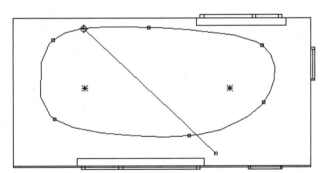

Fig. 11.22 The **Path** of the camera in the **Front (X/Y)** viewport

Notes

The animation sequences described in this chapter are all of a fairly simple nature. The possibilities of rendered animation with the aid of 3D Studio are almost without limit. It is hoped that the examples given here will encourage the reader to undertake further research and experimentation with the **Keyframer** program. There is, unfortunately, no space in a book of this nature to provide information on more intricate animations.

Questions

1. What do you understand by the term 'animation'?
2. What is a 'flic' file?
3. How does one determine the number of keys or segments in a **Keyframer** animation?
4. What is the meaning of the terms 'child', 'parent' and 'family' with respect to the hierarchy in a scene involving many objects in the **Keyframer**?
5. How is the frame segment in the **Keyframer** program set?
6. Why do you think it necessary to make frequent use of the **HOLD** button of the Icon panel when working in the **Keyframer** program?
7. What differences are there in the settings in the **Track Info:** dialogue box compared with the **Key Info:** dialogue box?
8. How does one ensure that an animation is saved to a file while its frames are being rendered?
9. When might it be necessary to leave a computer running to render an animation overnight?
10. In which dialogue box can one check the Family tree of a scene containing many objects?

Exercises

1. Fig. 8.22 on page 136 shows three meshing gears. If you have worked this example (the eighth example of Chapter 8), load the 3D mesh back into 3D Studio and create an animation in which the gears revolve with relation to each other.
2. The seventh example of Chapter 8 is a kitchen scene. Re-load the 3DS file for the scene and create a walk-through animation involving a path for the camera in the **Keyframer**.
3. Re-load the room project given as the fourth example in this chapter and add the chair from Exercise 2, Chapter 9, and the table of the fourth example in Chapter 8 in suitable positions in the room scene and create a walk-through animation involving the room, the chair and the table. The rendering may possibly take at least 2 hours even with a reasonably fast computer.

APPENDIX A

Glossary

This glossary contain some of the more common computing terms.

Application – the name given to software packages that perform tasks such as word processing, desktop publishing, CAD etc.

ASCII – american national standard code for information interchange. A code which assigns bits to characters used in computing.

AT – advanced technology. Applied to PCs which have an 80286 processor (or better).

Autodesk – the American company which produces AutoCAD and other CAD software packages.

BASIC – beginner's all-purpose symbolic instruction code. A programing language.

Baud rate – a measure of the rate at which a computer system can send and receive information (measured in bits per second).

BIOS – basic input/output system. The chip in a PC that controls the operations performed by the hardware (e.g. disks, screen, keyboard etc.)

Bit – short for binary digit. Binary is a form of mathematics that uses only two numbers: 0 and 1. Computers operate completely on binary mathematics.

Block – a group of objects or entities on screen that have been linked together to act as one unit.

Booting up – starting up a computer to an operating level.

Bus – an electronic channel that allows the movement of data around a computer.

Byte – a sequence of 8 bits.

C – a computer programing language.

Cache – a section of memory (can be ROM or RAM) which holds data that is being frequently used. Speeds up the action of disks and applications.

CAD – computer-aided design. Should not be used as computer-aided drawing.

CAD/CAM – computer-aided design and manufacturing.

CD-ROM – compact disc read only memory. A disk system capable of storing several hundred Mb of data – commonly 640 Mb. Data can only be read from a CD-ROM, not written to it.

CGA – colour graphic adaptor. A screen display with a resolution of 320 x 200 in four colours. Not used much with modern CAD systems.

Chips – pieces of silicon that have the electronic circuits that drive computers formed from other minerals on their surface.

Clock speed – usually measured in MHz (megahertz) – this is a measure of the speed at which a computer processor works.

Clone –refers to a PC that functions in a way identical to the original IBM PC.

CMOS – complementary metal oxide semiconductor. Often found as battery powered chips which control features such as the PC's clock speed.

Communications – describes the software and hardware that allow computers to communicate.

Compatible – generally used as a term for software able to run on any computer that is an IBM clone.

Coprocessor – a processor chip in a computer that runs in tandem with the main processor chip, and can deal with arithmetic involving many decimal points (floating-point arithmetic). Often used in CAD systems to speed up drawing operations.

CPU – central processing unit. The chip which drives a PC.

Data – information that is created, used or stored on computer in digital form.

Database – a piece of software that can handle and organize large amounts of information.

Directories – the system used in MS-DOS for organizing files on disk. Could be compared to a folder (the directory) containing documents (the files).

Disks – storage hardware for holding data (files, applications, etc.). There are many types; the most common are hard disks (for mass storage) and floppy disks (less storage) and CD-ROMs (mass storage).

Display – the screen allowing an operator to see the results of his work at a computer.

DOS – disk operating system. The software that allows the computer to access and organize stored data. MS-DOS (produced by the Microsoft Corporation) is the DOS most widely used in PCs.

DTP – desktop publishing. DTP software allows for the combination of text and graphics into page layouts, which may then be printed.

EGA – enhanced graphics adaptor. A screen display with a resolution of 640 x 350 pixels in 16 colours.

Entity – a single feature or graphic being drawn on screen, e.g. a line, a circle, a point, etc. Sometimes linked together with other entities to form a block, where the block then acts as a single entity.

EMS – expanded memory specification. RAM over and above the original limit of 640 Kb RAM in the original IBM PC. PCs are now being built to take up to 64 Mb RAM.

File – a collection of data held as an entity on a disk.

Fixed disk – a hard disk that cannot usually be easily removed from the computer; as distinct from floppy disks which are designed to be easily removable.

Floppy disk – a removable disk that stores data in magnetic form. The actual disk is a thin circular sheet of plastic with a magnetic surface, hence the term 'floppy'. It usually has a firm plastic case.

Formating – the process of preparing the magnetic surface of a disk to enable it to hold digital data.

Giga – means 1,000,000,000. In computer memory terms 1000 Mb (megabytes) – actually 1,073,741,824 bytes because there are 1024 bytes in a kilobyte (K).

GUI – graphical user interface. Describes software (such as Windows) which allows the user to control the computer by representing functions with icons and other graphical images.

Hardcopy – the result of printing (or plotting) text or graphics on to paper or card.

Hard disk – a disk, usually fixed in a computer, which rotates at high speed and will hold large amounts of data, often up to 1 gigabyte.

Hardware – the equipment used in computing: the computer itself, disks, printers, monitor, etc.

Hz (hertz) – the measure of 1 cycle per second. In computing terms, often used in millions of hertz (megahertz or MHz) as a measure of the clock speed.

IBM – International Business Machines. An American computer manufacturing company – the largest in the world.

Intel – an American company which manufactures the processing chips used in the majority of PCs.

Joystick – a small control unit used mainly for computer games. Some CAD systems use a joystick to control drawing on screen.

Kilo – means 1000. In computing terms 1 K (kilobyte) is 1024 bytes.

LAN – local area network. Describes a network that might typically link PCs in an office by cable, where distance between the PCs are small.

Library – a set of frequently used symbols, phrases or other data on disk, that can be easily accessed by the operator.

Light Pen – stylus used to point directly at a display screen sensitive to its use.

Memory – any medium (such as RAM or ROM chips) that allows the computer to store data internally that can be instantly recalled.

MHz – megahertz. 1,000,000 hertz (cycles per second).

Mouse – a device for controlling the position of an on-screen pointer within a GUI such as Windows.

Microcomputer – a PC is a microcomputer; a minicomputer is much larger and a mainframe computer is larger still. With the increase in memory possible with a microcomputer, the term seems to be dropping out of use.

Microsoft – the American company which produces the Windows and MS-DOS software.

MIPS – millions of instructions per second. A measure of a computer's speed – it is not comparable with the clock speed as measured in MHz because a single instruction may take more than a single cycle to perform.

Monitor – the computer's display screen.

MS-DOS – Microsoft Disk Operating System.

Multitasking – a computer that can carry out more than one task at the same time is said to be multitasking. For example, in AutoCAD for Windows, printing can be carried out 'in the background' while a new drawing is being constructed.

Multiuser – a computer that may be used by more than one operator.

Networking – the joining together of a group of computers, allowing them to share the same data and software applications. LANs and WANs are examples of the types of networks available.

Object – a term used in CAD to describe an entity, or a group of entities that have been linked together.

Operating system – software, and in some cases hardware, that allows the user to operate applications software and organize and use data stored on a computer.

PC – personal computer. Should strictly only be used to refer to an IBM clone, but is now in general use.

Pixels – the individual dots of a computer display.

Plotter – produces hardcopy of, for instance, a drawing produced on computer by moving a pen over a piece of paper or card.

Printer – there are many types of printer; dot-matrix, bubble-jet and laser are the most common. Allows material produced on computer (graphics and text) to be output as hardcopy.

Processor – the operating chip of a PC. Usually a single chip, such as the Intel 80386 or 80486 chip.

Programs – a set of instructions to the computer that has been designed to produce a given result.

RAM – random access memory. Data stored in RAM is lost when the computer is switched off, unless previously saved to a disk.

RGB – red, green, blue.

RISC – reduced instruction set chip. A very fast processor.

ROM – read only memory. Refers to those chips from which the data stored can be read but to which data cannot be written are not lost when the computer is switched off.

Scanner – hardware capable of being passed over a document or drawing and reading the image into a computer.

Software – refers to any program or application that is used and run on computer.

SQL – structured query language.

UNIX – a multiuser, multitasking operating system (short for UNICS: uniplexed information and computing system).

VDU – visual display unit.

Vectors – refers to entities in computer graphics which are defined by the end points of each part of the entity.

VGA – video graphics array. Screen displays with a resolution of up to 640 x 480 pixels in 256 colours. SVGA (Super VGA) allows resolutions of up to 1024 x 768 pixels.

Virtual memory – a system by which disk space is used to allow the computer to function as if more physical RAM were present. It is used by Windows (and other software), but can slow down a computer's operation.

WAN – wide area network. A network of computers that are a large distance apart – communication is often done down telephone lines.

Weitek – makers of math coprocessor chips for 80386 and 80486 computers. Important for AutoCAD users, because the addition of a Weitek coprocessor chip speeds up drawing construction processes considerably.

WIMP – windows, icons, mice and pointers. A term that is used to describe some GUIs.

Winchesters – hard disks. Refers to the company which made the first hard disks. An out-of-date term.

Window – an area of the computer screen within which applications such as word processors may be operated.

Workstation – often used to refer to a multiuser PC, or other system used for the purposes of CAD (or other applications).

WORM – write once, read many. An optical storage system that allows blank optical disks to have data written onto them only once.

WYSIWYG – what you see is what you get. What is seen on the screen is what will be printed.

XMS – extended memory specifications. RAM above the 1Mb limit.

XT – extended technology. Was used to refer to the original 8060- or 8088-based computers.

MS-DOS

Introduction

This book introduces the use of the software Autodesk 3D Studio – i.e. with the 3D Studio software installed in a 386, 486 or Pentium computer running under MS-DOS. In this chapter some information regarding commands in MS-DOS as they may affect the use of 3D Studio are briefly described. Although 3D Studio will run with any MS-DOS system from version 3.3 onwards, its best performance will be with MS-DOS version 5.0 (or higher). MS-DOS is an abbreviation for Microsoft Disk Operating System. Microsoft is an American software company. MS-DOS is a complex program and this chapter gives only a very brief summary of a few of the numerous commands available with the program.

Start-up

When a personal computer (PC) running under MS-DOS is switched on a self-test is run – memory, system circuits, disk drives and other peripherals are checked. When the PC is satisfied that these are OK, some of the MS-DOS files are loaded into memory. At this stage only those commands most frequently used are loaded. Commands not used so often are loaded as and when they are required.

The PC may have several drives – see Fig. B.1. The working files of 3D Studio must be loaded onto a hard disk, so in the example given in Fig. B.1, the files will be on drive C:. PCs may have more drives than those shown in Fig.B.1 – up to as many as 26 are possible working under MS-DOS, although it is more usual to have four or five – e.g. floppy disk drives A: and B:, Hard disk drives C: and D: and perhaps a CD-ROM drive E:.

When the start-up test procedure is completed, a series of statements may appear on screen, usually finishing with the MS-DOS command line prompt **C:\>**. MS-DOS commands are entered at this prompt. With MS-DOS version 5.0, it is possible to have the start-up

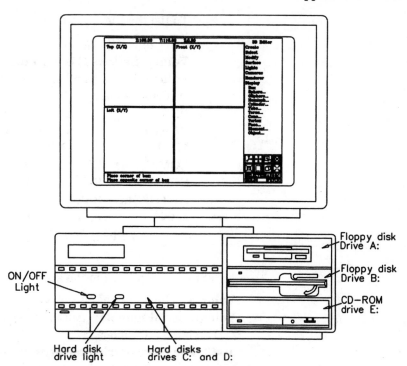

Fig. B.1 A typical PC set-up such as would be used at a 3D Studio workstation

showing a graphics screen from which commands, etc., can be selected with the aid of a mouse. Here we will only be concerned with commands entered from the keyboard.

When a PC is switched on from the power switch, this is said to be a *cold start*. When the computer has been running for some time, if a fault occurs a *warm start* can be made by pressing the three keys Ctrl/Alt/Del simultaneously. It is advisable to avoid too many cold starts when using a PC, because repeated cold starts may damage the chips in the system circuits. Warm starts do not carry this risk. Avoid warm starts while working in 3D Studio if possible. A good practice in any case is to save your work at regular intervals – say every 15 minutes or so. Then if anything goes wrong – e.g. a fault in the power supply – at least most of your work will have been saved.

Some MS-DOS commands

Capital or lower case letters can be used for any of the MS-DOS commands.

To change from drive C: to drive A:

C:\\> *enter* a: *Return*
A:\\>

Drive A: becomes the current drive.

To list the files on a disk

C:\\> *enter* dir　*Return*
Volume in drive C is hard-disk
Volume Serial Number is 1AC3-5075
Directory of C:

DOS	<DIR>		20/10/91	17:18
ACAD12	<DIR>		19/08/92	11:25
3DS3	<DIR>		21/01/94	10:04
COMMAND	COM	175	19/06/93	9:35
CONFIG	SYS	307	19/06/93	10:53
AUTOEXEC	BAT	332	19/06/93	10:59
WIN	BAT	8	05/08/93	8:47

　　　　　7 file(s)　　　　　　**1822 bytes**
　　　　　　　　　　　　　38178240 bytes free

Taking examples from the above directory:

Volume: The name that is given to the hard disk by the operator.

Volume serial number: Automatically given to a disk by MS-DOS version 5.0 (or later).

3DS3: The name of the directory holding the 3D Studio Release 3.

<DIR>: Shows that this is the name of a directory.

19/08/93: Shows that the directory was made on the 19th August 1993.

11:25 is the time of the day (24 hour clock) when the directory or file was saved to disk.

AUTOEXEC　BAT: **AUTOEXEC** is the name of a file with **BAT** being the file extension.

WIN　BAT: An example of what is known as a *batch file*. In this example entering *win* at the DOS prompt **C:\\>** starts up the Windows software.

332: Against the file name and its extension, this is the size of the file in bytes.

To list files in a directory

C:\\> *enter* dir 3ds3　*Return*

Will give a list of all sub-directories and files in the directory 3DS3. Because the number of files in the directory 3DS3 is greater than the screen can show, the following will list the files screen by screen:

C:\\> dir ds3/p *Return*

Directories and sub-directories

Fig. B.2 shows the structure of the MS-DOS disk filing hierarchy. In Fig. B2, some examples of the meanings of the names in are:

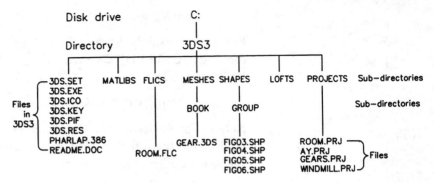

Fig. B.2 The MS-DOS
directory and part of the
files structure of the
directory 3DS3

C: is the name of the drive holding the directories and files.

3DS3 is the name of the directory holding the 3D Studio directories
and files.

MATLIBS is the sub-directory of 3DS3, holding the material libraries.

MESHES is the sub-directory of 3DS3 in which my 3D meshes created
in 3D Studio are held.

BOOK is the sub-directory of MESHES in which the 3D meshes for this
book are held.

SHAPES is the sub-directory of 3DS3 in which the shape files created
in the 2D Shaper program are held.

GROUP is the sub-directory of SHAPES holding the shape files for
some figures in this book.

LOFTS is the sub-directory of 3DS3 holding the loft files created in the
3D Lofter program.

PROJECTS is the sub-directory of 3DS3 holding project files.

To make a directory

C:\\> *enter* md (*or* mkdir) 3ds3

The directory **3DS3** is formed on drive **C:**.

To change directories

C:\\> *enter* cd 3ds3 *Return*
C:\\3DS3\\>

The current directory is changed to the **3DS3** sub-directory.

To make a sub-directory in 3DS3

C:\\3DS3\\> *enter* md book *Return*

The directory **BOOK** is created as a sub-directory of **3DS3**.

Working with files

File names usually have a file extension. The file **ROOM** in sub-directory **3DS3/PROJECTS** will have a file name extension **.prj**. Thus its full name is:

3DS3\PROJECTS\ROOM.PRJ

Note the back-slashes between directory and sub-directories (or file names) and the full stop after the file name and before its extension. These are obligatory.

File name extensions

Autodesk 3D Studio 3 recognises a fair number of different types of files, with a variety of file name extensions – the three (usually) letters after the full stop in a file name. This is because the software loads, manipulates and creates graphics and a large number of different types of graphics file formats have been developed during recent years. Some are special to 3DS Studio. Some are derived from other graphics software packages, but can be loaded into 3D Studio. Among those the beginner is likely to come across are the following:

.exe A file which executes a software progam (also the **.com** extension). An example is **3ds.exe** held in the directory **3ds**. When the **3ds.exe** file is called it loads into memory and 3D Studio starts up.

.3ds 3D Studio 3D mesh file (created within **3D Editor**).

.bak A backup file. If a 3D Studio 3D mesh file is saved more than once a backup file (with the **.bak** extension) is automatically created on disk.

.shp 3D Studio shape file (created within **2D Shaper**).

.lft 3D Studio loft file (created within **3D Lofter**).

.flc 3D Studio animation file (created within **Keyframer**).

.prj 3D Studio project file containing all the related data for a scene.

.set 3D Studio configuration file.

.fnt 3D Studio font file.

.dxf An AutoCAD (or other CAD package) data exchange file.

.tga A graphics bitmap file.

.tif A graphics bitmap file.

.gif A graphics bitmap file.

.bmp A graphics bitmap file.

.flm A filmroll file created in AutoCAD.

.fli A graphics file created within Autodesk Animator.

.cel   A graphics file created within Autodesk Animator.

.pfb   A Postscript font file.

To copy a file from one directory to another

C:\> copy 3ds3\projects\room.prj d:\room.prj

The file **room.prj** is copied from the **3ds3\projects** sub-directory on the C: hard disk onto the D: hard disk.

To copy a number of files between directories

C:\> copy 3ds3\projects*.* d:\new

Copies all files in the directory **c:\3ds3\projects** to the directory **new** on the hard disk D:. The asterisk * is known as a *wildcard* and in computer terms really means 'all'.

To rename a file

C:\> rename 3ds3\projects\room.prj 3ds3\projects\kitchen.prj

renames the file **room.prj** as **kitchen.prj**.

To erase a file

C:\> erase (*or* del) 3ds\projects\room.prj

The file **room.prj** is deleted from the disk.

Note: Take great care when erasing. If a backup file (extension .bak) has replaced the erased file, it will be possible to rename it to the file name it is backing up. Otherwise a file may be lost. MS-DOS version 5.0 does however have an **UNDELETE** command, which may save such a situation. For example:

C:\> undelete 3ds\projects

will list all files in the directory **3ds/projects** which have been erased. The erased files will have a ? replacing the first letter of the erased files. Enter a letter to replace the lost first letter and the file will become un-erased. This does not always work, because another file may have filled the sectors on the disk from which the erased file had been deleted if any work has been done after the erasure. If this has happened the erased file cannot be recovered with the **undelete** command.

Keyboard short-cuts

Introduction

Autodesk 3D Studio can be operated almost entirely by relying on keyboard short-cuts – i.e. by the selection of commands by entering letters or a combination of letters and keystrokes from the keyboard. Many of these short-cuts will be seen against command names in the illustrations of pull-down menus which have appeared in this book. A list of those short-cuts most likely to be of value to the beginner with the software is given below; it must be realised that this is not a complete list.

Keyboard short-cuts

Pressing a single key

Esc	Cancel process.
	Cancel a rendering.
	Undo the last action in either the **2D Shaper** or **3D Lofter**.
Tab	Toggles the directions of the unidirectional cursor.
Q	Quit a program.
Y	Yes, do as is asked in the message box.
N	No, do not do as asked in the message box.
?	Current status of program.
!	Redraw the window in current use.
S	Snap set in the current viewport – **S** appears top right of screen.
G	Grid set in the current viewport – Grid dots appear.
A	Use angle snap in the current viewport – **A** appears top right of screen.

Selection of viewing position in the viewport

B	Bottom view.
T	Top view.

C   Camera view.
F   Front view.
L   View from left.
R   View from right.
U   User view.

Function key-strokes

F1   Switch to the **2D Shaper** program.
F2   Switch to the **3D Lofter** program.
F3   Switch to the **3D Editor** program.
F4   Switch to the **Keyframer** program.
F5   Switch to the **Materials Editor** program.
F10   Switch to the DOS.

Pressing the Ctrl key plus another

Ctrl/H   Same as a *left-click* on the **HOLD** button in an icon panel.
Ctrl/F   Same as a *left-click* on the **FETCH** button in an icon panel.
Ctrl/A   Brings up the **Snap Spacing:** dialogue box, in which **Snap**, **Grid** and **Angle** spacings can be set.

Zoom key combinations

Shift/Z   Zoom in.
Ctrl/Z   Zoom viewport extents.
Z   Zoom out.
Alt/Z   Select zoom window with mouse.

Index